Baking

FOR EVERY SEASON

photography by

ERIN SCOTT

weldon**owen**

contents

INTRODUCTION — 9

FOLLOW THE SEASONS — 10

TIPS FOR BETTER BAKING — 14

spring

Lavender Shortbread — 18

Strawberry-Pecan Thumbprints — 19

Chocolate-Dipped Coconut-Almond Macaroons — 20

Apricot-Pistachio Rugelach — 22

Mexican Wedding Cookies — 23

Mini Cream Scones with Fresh Strawberry Jam — 25

Hot Cross Buns — 26

Rose & Vanilla Bean Tea Cakes — 27

Rhubarb Turnovers — 28

Beignets — 30

Cherry Clafoutis — 31

Apricot Mascarpone Crostata — 33

Spring Strawberry Tart with Orange Cream — 34

Strawberry-Rhubarb Breakfast Cake — 35

Sour Cherry Pot Pies — 36

Mini Red Velvet Cupcakes with Cream Cheese Frosting — 38

Strawberry Cheesecake Cupcakes — 39

Crème Brûlée Tartlets — 41

Coconut Lime Curd Layer Cake — 42

Passion Fruit Cupcakes with Coconut Frosting — 44

Orange Vanilla Bean Sponge Cake with Sugared Strawberries — 47

Bittersweet Chocolate Almond Torte — 49

Angel Food Cake with Strawberry-Rhubarb Compote — 50

Carrot Cake — 52

King Cake — 53

summer

Blackberry Cobbler — 56

Lemon Crinkle Cookies — 58

Dulce de Leche Alfajores — 59

Lime Curd Coconut Bars — 61

Plum Jam Oatmeal Streusel Bars — 62

Caramel Orange Flan — 63

Blueberry Cheesecake Squares with Hazelnut Crust — 64

Apricot-Almond Crisp — 66

Peach Streusel Pie — 67

Honey Pistachio Baklava — 69

Lemon Meringue Pie with Gingersnap Crust — 70

Cherry Lattice Pie — 71

Cinnamon-Sugar Churros — 72

Honey-Nectarine Cheesecake — 74

Blueberry-Lemon Drizzle Cake — 75

Strawberry Shortcakes — 77

Piñata Cupcakes — 78

Chocolate Mint Chip Ice Cream Cake — 79

Summer Peach-Raspberry Muffins — 80

Vanilla Ombré Layer Cake — 82

Summer Fruit Trifle — 85

Tres Leches Cake — 86

Red, White & Blue Bundt Cake — 87

Triple-Decker Birthday Cake — 88

Berries & Cream Roulade — 89

fall

Pumpkin Whoopie Pies — 93

Caramelized Pear Ginger Cake — 94

Oatmeal Pear Crisp — 95

Pistachio Brittle — 96

Maple Pumpkin Pie — 98

Caramel Cranberry-Almond Tart — 99

Chocolate, Cherry & Hazelnut Biscotti — 101

Classic Pecan Pie — 102

White Chocolate Grasshopper Pie — 103

Apple-Ginger Tart with Cider-Bourbon Sauce — 104

Honey-Nut Pie — 106

Classic Tarte Tatin — 107

Butterscotch-Bourbon Pie 109

Almond-Jam Cakes 110

Pumpkin Chocolate Chip Cupcakes 111

Devil's Food Chocolate Cupcakes 112

Bread & Butter Pudding
with Marmalade 114

Sweet Potato Corn Bread 115

Cranberry Upside-Down Cake 117

Pumpkin Coffee Cake with
Pecan Streusel 118

Challah 119

Cinnamon Rolls 120

winter

Meyer Lemon Curd Pavlova with
Blood Oranges & Cream 125

Almond Cookies 126

Hot Cocoa Cookies 127

Peppermint Bark Brownies 128

Peppermint Swirl Macarons 130

Gingerbread Cutout Cookies 132

Chocolate, Raspberry & Toasted
Almond Bark 133

Chocolate-Raspberry Mini Tarts 135

S'mores Fudge 136

Chocolate-Hazelnut Pastry Wreath 137

Raspberry Linzer Hearts 138

Chestnut Torte with Mocha
Buttercream 140

Sweet Potato Pie with
Pecan Streusel 141

Pear-Almond Custard Tart 142

Bittersweet Chocolate &
Salted Caramel Tart 145

Spiced Apple Strudel 146

Blood Orange Tartlets 147

Mini Lemon Poppyseed
Drizzle Cakes 148

Chocolate Espresso Heart Cake 150

Mocha Bûche de Noël 151

Steamed Figgy Pudding 152

Sticky Toffee Pudding 153

Chocolate Florentines 155

Spiced Apple Honey Cake 156

Warm Molten Chocolate Cakes 157

Chocolate Babka 158

Panettone 160

BASIC RECIPES

Sugar Cookies 164

Chocolate Sugar Cookies 165

Flaky Pie Dough, Single Crust 166

Flaky Pie Dough, Double Crust 166

Tart Dough 167

Cocoa Tart Dough 167

Cream Cheese Tartlet Dough 168

Wafer Cookie Crust 168

Gingersnap Crust 169

Chocolate Ganache 169

Vanilla Icing 170

Royal Icing 170

Fluffy Vanilla Frosting 171

Fudge Frosting 171

Chocolate Frosting 172

White Chocolate Frosting 172

Cream Cheese Frosting 173

Whipped Honey Frosting 173

Quick Vanilla Buttercream 174

Vanilla Meringue Buttercream 174

Coconut Buttercream 175

Mocha Buttercream 175

Whipped Cream 176

Vanilla Bean Pastry Cream 176

Lemon Curd 177

Lime Curd 177

INDEX

INDEX 179

introduction

Freshly baked bread and its warm, buttery aroma on a chilly autumn day, spiced gingerbread cookies perfect for a winter gathering, springtime strawberries and rhubarb simmered into a cake-topping compote, and fresh summer peaches bubbling in a streusel-topped pie for a backyard barbecue—all of these tributes are inextricably tied to specific times of the year. Baking is naturally seasonal, conjuring childhood memories of summer fun, the nostalgia of winter holidays, the first growth of spring, and the abundance of the fall harvest.

While produce might be available year-round, the best fruits and vegetables are found at the peak of their season. With more than 100 recipes for making the best use of those ingredients, *Baking for Every Season* leads you through spring, summer, fall, and winter with baking ideas for everyday treats and every special occasion. The flavors and spices identified with each season are highlighted in both classic and updated desserts and baked goods, each of them worthy of a celebration and ideal for the time of year.

Creating lasting memories in the kitchen is often synonymous with celebrating the holidays together, when families and friends gather. A multilayered cake for a birthday, a tres leches cake for Cinco de Mayo, an apple-ginger tart for Thanksgiving, honey pistachio baklava for Eid, hot cross buns for Easter, sweet potato corn bread for Kwanzaa, or peppermint bark brownies for Christmas are all delicious ways to rejoice and take part in seasonal festivities.

The seasonal-fruit guide showcases what to look for in star produce, from apricots and cherries to pears and Meyer lemons. Plus, invaluable baking tips give home bakers of all skill levels the information they need to take their creations to the next level.

follow the seasons

The following seasonal categories list fruits according to their season of peak ripeness. Some are available only in the early or late half of a season, and some year-round.

YEAR-ROUND

Apples (best in late summer and fall), bananas, grapefruits, lemons (best from fall to spring), limes (best in spring), oranges (best from fall to spring), pineapples (best from spring to summer)

SPRING

Apricots (available in late spring), blueberries, cherries (available in late spring), plums (available in late spring), raspberries (available in late spring), rhubarb (field rhubarb is not available until late spring), strawberries, tangerines

SUMMER

Apricots, blueberries, cherries (available in early summer), figs, grapes (available in late summer), mangoes, melons, nectarines (white and yellow), pears (some varieties are available in late summer), plums, rhubarb

FALL

Cranberries, figs (available in early fall), grapes, kiwifruits, mangoes (available in early fall), papayas, pears, persimmons, tangerines

WINTER

Cranberries, dates, kiwifruits, pears, tangerines, blood oranges

choosing seasonal fruits

Try to buy fruits that are in season, locally grown, and, ideally, organic. You will be rewarded with succulent, juicy, fragrant fruits that are full of flavor and sweetness, and that are generally lower in cost than out-of-season produce. A local farmers' market is your best bet for the most in-season produce. Some fruits, such as apples, are available throughout the year because some varieties come into season as others go out or because imported fruits fill store bins. Most fruits, however, have a limited growing season.

APPLES & PEARS

Apples and pears, each with scores of varieties, are two of the baker's favorite fruits. Among the best crisp-tart baking apples are Rome Beauty, Baldwin, Gravenstein, Pink Lady, Northern Spy, Winesap, Granny Smith, Royal Gala, and McIntosh. Bartlett (Williams), Anjou, and Bosc are among the best pears for baking. Choose fragrant fruits that are unblemished. Pears should yield slightly to the touch.

BERRIES

Plump, juicy berries, such as raspberries, blackberries, blueberries, boysenberries, strawberries, and others, flourish in summer. When choosing berries, look for fresh, shiny fruits that are dry and free of mold, and smell delicious.

CITRUS

Lemons, limes, oranges, and grapefruits are the primary citrus fruits for baking. Within these broad groups are many specialized varieties, such as Meyer lemons, Key limes, and blood oranges. Most parts of the fruits—juice, peel, zest, flesh—are used, but avoid using the bitter white pith just below the fragrant layer of peel. Choose heavy fruits with shiny skins. If a recipe calls for citrus juice, always use freshly squeezed.

STONE FRUITS

This family of fruit loves hot summer days. Stone fruits have a single center pit, known as the stone, and include peaches, nectarines, plums, cherries, and apricots. They can either be freestone, meaning the fruit slips easily from the stone, or cling, meaning the fruit is firmly attached to the pit. The best stone fruits are juicy, fragrant, and sweet. Choose heavy, unblemished fruits that yield slightly to the touch.

DRIED FRUITS

Dried fruits, such as raisins, currants, cherries, cranberries, and figs, are excellent sources of texture and flavor. Look for moist dried fruits that feel soft when pressed. To ensure freshness, purchase only as much as you need. Seek out unsulfured organic dried fruits for better flavor. Store dried fruits in an airtight container at room temperature for up to 1 month, or in the refrigerator for up to 3 months.

tips for better baking

Close your eyes and imagine serving a warm caramelized pear ginger cake after a winter holiday feast. Or presenting a child with an ice cream cake for their summer birthday party. A platter of mini cream scones for a springtime tea party and devil's food chocolate cupcakes for a wicked Halloween are just two more delicious reasons to get in the kitchen and start baking with the seasons. Here are some suggestions for achieving the best results.

READ THE RECIPE

Read through the recipe before you start and make sure you have all the ingredients. Be sure that the timing works for your schedule—some recipes need to be prepped in advance or chilled overnight.

PREHEAT THE OVEN

Make sure to preheat your oven 15 minutes prior to baking. It's also a good idea to use an oven thermometer to make sure that your oven heats to the correct temperature. All of the recipes in this book were tested using a conventional oven, not a convection oven; if you have convection, reduce the temperature by 25°F (3°C).

USE GOOD-QUALITY INGREDIENTS

Fresh fruits that are fragrant and at the peak of their season will shine in your desserts and baked goods. Similarly, organic or chemical-free produce will always yield deeper flavors and tastier results than produce that is out of season and conventional. Seek out good-quality brands of unsalted butter, unbleached organic flour, organic and cage-free eggs, nuts from a high turnover bulk bin, fresh spices, and high-end chocolate, as these ingredients will make a big difference in your results.

ADD A PINCH OF SALT

A little bit of salt enhances the sweetness and natural flavors in your baked goods. Look for a good-quality fine sea salt rather than using iodized salt. Kosher salt is also terrific in baking, and is less "salty" than fine sea salt, so you can use a tiny bit more if you like.

KNOW WHEN TO KEEP YOUR HANDS OFF

Quick breads, like scones and corn bread, and pastry dough, such as tart and pie dough, are best if you don't overmix them. The same is true of cake and muffin batters. When you stir or knead flour, you create gluten strands, which is terrific if you are making a yeasted dough like challah (the gluten strands add structure). But for a tender crumb or flaky pastry, you want to minimize gluten, which will make your baked goods more dense.

TOP TOOLS FOR BAKING

- Measuring cups and spoons
- Mixing bowls
- Heatproof silicone spatula and wooden spoon
- Large and small whisks
- Fine-mesh sieve
- Electric or stand mixer with whisk and paddle attachments
- Rimmed half-sheet baking sheets
- Heavy-duty baking pans, such as two 9-inch round cake pans and an 8-inch square pan
- 9-inch square and 9-by-13-inch rectangular glass baking dishes
- Wire cooling racks

spring

lavender shortbread

These simple buttery shortbreads are subtly fragranced with fresh lavender. Be sure to select culinary lavender whenever cooking with lavender, which you can often find at organic markets or specialty-food stores. The best type of lavender for edibles are English lavender varieties.

2 cups (9 oz/240 g)
all-purpose flour

½ cup (2 oz/60 g) cornstarch

¼ teaspoon salt

1 cup (8 oz/225 g)
unsalted butter

½ cup (3½ oz/100 g) sugar

2 tablespoons finely chopped
unsprayed fresh or dried
English lavender flowers

MAKES 12 SHORTBREADS

Preheat the oven to 350°F (180°C). Have ready a 9½-inch (24-cm) round tart pan with a removable bottom.

In a bowl, sift together the flour, cornstarch, and salt. In a large bowl, using an electric mixer on medium speed, beat the butter and sugar until smooth and creamy, about 4 minutes. Add the lavender and beat well to combine. Slowly add the dry ingredients and beat on low speed just until the dough forms large clumps and pulls away from the sides of the bowl.

Press the dough evenly into the tart pan with a rubber spatula, then smooth the top. Using a fork, prick the entire surface of the dough, making holes about every ½ inch (12 mm) that are about ¼ inch (6 mm) deep. Place the pan on a baking sheet and bake until very lightly golden, 45–50 minutes.

While the shortbread is still hot, using a sharp knife, cut into 12 wedges. Set on a wire rack to cool in the pan, then remove the pan sides.

strawberry-pecan thumbprints

Vanilla-scented butter cookies get a toasty note from the addition of finely chopped pecans. Fresh strawberries are at their sweet peak in springtime, and you can easily transform them into homemade strawberry jam (see page 25). If you like, substitute another jam flavor for the strawberry, like apricot or sour cherry.

2 cups (9 oz/240 g) all-purpose flour

¼ teaspoon salt

1 cup (8 oz/225 g) unsalted butter, at cool room temperature

½ cup (3½ oz/100 g) sugar

1 large egg yolk

1 teaspoon vanilla extract

1 cup (4 oz/115 g) finely chopped toasted pecans

¼ cup (3 oz/70 g) strawberry jam, store-bought or homemade (page 25)

MAKES ABOUT 20 COOKIES

Preheat the oven to 325°F (165°C). Line a baking sheet with parchment paper.

In a bowl, sift together the flour and salt. In a large bowl, using an electric mixer on medium speed, beat the butter and sugar until well blended, about 1 minute. Reduce the speed to low, add the egg yolk and vanilla, and beat until the yolk is completely incorporated. Slowly add the flour mixture and beat on low speed just until incorporated.

Put the pecans in a small bowl. Scoop up a rounded tablespoon of the dough and roll between your palms into a ball. Lightly roll the ball in the pecans to coat completely and place on the prepared sheet. Repeat with the remaining dough, spacing the balls about 2 inches (5 cm) apart.

Using a thumb, press an indentation about ¼ inch (6 mm) deep in the center of each cookie. Spoon about ½ teaspoon jam into each indentation. Bake until the bottoms and edges of the cookies are lightly browned, 20–25 minutes.Transfer the baking sheet to a wire rack and let the cookies cool on the sheet for about 5 minutes, then transfer the cookies to the rack to cool completely, about 30 minutes longer. Serve.

chocolate-dipped coconut-almond macaroons

Toasted mounds of shredded coconut and plenty of almonds pack a lot of flavor into these naturally gluten-free cookies that are a favorite for Passover. The crunchy-on-the-outside, chewy-on-the-inside texture is irresistible, and made even better after a dip in melted chocolate.

3½ cups (14 oz/420 g)
sweetened shredded
dried coconut

1 cup (3 oz/90 g)
sliced almonds

½ cup (5½ oz/155 g)
sweetened condensed milk

½ teaspoon almond extract

2 large egg whites

1 tablespoon sugar

¼ teaspoon salt

1 cup (6 oz/170 g)
chocolate chips, melted

MAKES ABOUT 18 COOKIES

Preheat the oven to 350°F (180°C). Line 2 baking sheets with parchment paper. On one baking sheet, combine 1½ cups (6 oz/180 g) of the coconut and the almonds. Toast the coconut and almonds in the oven, stirring occasionally, until golden, about 12 minutes. Remove from the oven and let cool completely.

In a large bowl, combine the cooled coconut mixture, the remaining 2 cups (8 oz/240 g) coconut, condensed milk, and almond extract. In another large bowl, using an electric mixer on high speed, beat together the egg whites, sugar, and salt until soft peaks form. Using a rubber spatula, gently fold the egg whites into the coconut mixture.

Using a large spoon, form mounds 2 inches (5 cm) in diameter on the prepared sheets, spacing them 3 inches (7.5 cm) apart. Bake until the cookies are golden brown, about 10 minutes. Transfer to racks and let cool completely. Reserve the baking sheets lined with parchment.

Dip the bottoms of the cookies into the melted chocolate and transfer chocolate-side down to the prepared baking sheets. Refrigerate until the chocolate is set.

apricot-pistachio rugelach

A flaky cream cheese dough is the base for these jam-and-nut-filled crescents. They are often served at Jewish holiday celebrations, like Rosh Hashanah. This variation features apricot jam and roasted pistachios. Brush the cookies with an egg white glaze and sprinkle with sugar before baking.

FOR THE DOUGH

1 cup (8 oz/225 g) unsalted butter, at cool room temperature

½ lb (250 g) cream cheese, at room temperature

¼ teaspoon salt

2 cups (9 oz/240 g) all-purpose flour, plus more for dusting

FOR THE FILLING

½ cup (6 oz/160 g) apricot preserves

½ cup (3 oz/85 g) finely chopped dried apricots

½ cup (1¾ oz/50 g) finely chopped unsalted pistachios

FOR THE TOPPING

¼ cup (1¾ oz/50 g) sugar

¾ teaspoon ground cinnamon

1 large egg white, lightly beaten with 1 teaspoon water

MAKES 48 COOKIES

To make the dough, in a large bowl, using an electric mixer on medium-high speed, beat the butter and cream cheese until smooth, about 1 minute. Mix in the salt. Stop the mixer and scrape down the sides of the bowl with a rubber spatula. Add the flour and mix on low speed just until a dough forms.

Turn the dough out onto a lightly floured work surface. Using floured hands, form the dough into a log. Cut the dough into 4 equal portions and flatten each portion into a disk. Wrap each disk separately in plastic wrap and refrigerate until firm, at least 2 hours or up to overnight.

Preheat the oven to 375°F (190°C). Line 2 baking sheets with parchment paper.

Let the dough disks stand at room temperature for about 10 minutes to soften slightly.

To make the filling, in a bowl, stir together the apricot preserves, dried apricots, and pistachios.

Lightly flour 1 dough disk and place between 2 sheets of parchment paper. Using a rolling pin, roll out the dough into a 10-inch (25-cm) round about ⅛ inch (3 mm) thick. Remove the top sheet of parchment and spread with one-fourth of the apricot mixture evenly over the round. Using a large knife, cut the round into 12 wedges. Starting at the wide end of the wedge, gently roll up each wedge to the point. Transfer the rolled wedges to a prepared baking sheet, arranging them point side down and 1 inch (2.5 cm) apart. Repeat with the remaining dough disks and filling.

To make the topping, in a small bowl, stir together the sugar and cinnamon. Brush the cookies evenly with the egg white mixture, then sprinkle generously with the cinnamon–sugar mixture.

Bake until golden brown, about 20 minutes. Transfer the baking sheets to wire racks and let cool for 5 minutes, then transfer the rugelach to the racks and let cool completely.

mexican wedding cookies

Also known as snowballs and Russian tea cakes, these melt-in-your-mouth cookies are traditionally wrapped in tissue paper and served at weddings and other celebrations in Mexico. You can substitute a different nut, such as pecans or walnuts, in the same amount, or leave the nuts out altogether.

1¾ cups (7½ oz/210 g) all-purpose flour

1 teaspoon ground cinnamon

1 cup (8 oz/225 g) unsalted butter, at cool room temperature

1½ cups (6 oz/185 g) confectioners' sugar

1 teaspoon vanilla extract

¼ teaspoon salt

1 cup (4 oz/115 g) finely chopped blanched almonds

MAKES 48 COOKIES

Preheat the oven to 350°F (180°C). Line a baking sheet with parchment paper.

In a bowl, sift together the flour and cinnamon. Set aside.

In another bowl, using an electric mixer on high speed, beat the butter until fluffy and pale, about 3 minutes. Add ½ cup (2 oz/60 g) of the sugar and beat until light and fluffy, about 2 minutes. Reduce the speed to low, add the vanilla and salt, and beat until combined, about 1 minute. Stop the mixer and scrape down the sides of the bowl. Add the flour mixture and beat on low speed until combined, about 1 minute. Stop the mixer and stir in the almonds.

Cover the bowl and refrigerate until the dough is chilled but not hard and is no longer sticky to the touch, about 15 minutes.

Shape the dough into 1-inch (2.5-cm) balls and place on the prepared baking sheet, spacing the cookies about 1 inch (2.5 cm) apart.

Bake until the cookies are just golden on the bottom, 10–12 minutes. Transfer the baking sheet to a wire rack and let the cookies cool on the sheet for 5 minutes.

Meanwhile, sift the remaining 1 cup (4 oz/115 g) sugar into a shallow bowl. Roll the cookies one at a time in the confectioners' sugar, place on the rack, and let cool completely.

mini cream scones with fresh strawberry jam

Bite-sized, flaky English-style scones are more tender and biscuit-like than American scones. The cream adds richness to this dough, but you could use an equal amount of buttermilk instead; just add ¼ teaspoon baking soda along with the baking powder. If you like, stir in ¼ cup (1½ oz/40 g) dried currants once you've added the cream.

FOR THE
STRAWBERRY JAM

2 pints (1 lb/500 g)
fresh strawberries,
hulled and chopped

1 cup (7 oz/200 g) sugar

2 tablespoons fresh
lemon juice

FOR THE CREAM SCONES

2 cups (9 oz/240 g)
all-purpose flour,
plus more for dusting

3 tablespoons sugar

2 teaspoons baking powder

½ teaspoon salt

½ cup (4 oz/115 g) cold
unsalted butter, cut into
small pieces

1 cup (250 ml) heavy cream,
plus more for brushing

**MAKES ABOUT 20 MINI SCONES
AND ABOUT 2 CUPS JAM**

To make the jam, place a saucer in the freezer to chill. In a saucepan over medium heat, combine the strawberries, sugar, and lemon juice and bring to a boil, stirring constantly to dissolve the sugar. Reduce the heat to medium-low and cook, uncovered, stirring occasionally, until the berries are tender and the juices thicken, about 10 minutes. To test for doneness, drop a small amount of jam onto the frozen saucer; if the liquid thickens to a jam-like consistency in about 20 seconds, it is ready. If it doesn't, continue to cook for a few minutes longer. Remove from the heat and let cool completely. Transfer the jam to jars and store in the refrigerator for up to 3 weeks.

To make the scones, preheat the oven to 400°F (200°C). Line a baking sheet with parchment paper.

In a food processor, combine the flour, sugar, baking powder, and salt and pulse until blended. Scatter the butter over the top and pulse until the butter is about the size of small peas. Add the cream and process just until the dough clumps together; it should be thick but moist.

Turn the dough out onto a floured work surface and gently press it together to form a mass, then flatten the dough into a disk about ½ inch (12 mm) thick. Using a 2-inch (5-cm) round biscuit cutter, cut out as many rounds as possible. Place the rounds on the prepared baking sheet, spacing them evenly apart. Gather up the dough scraps, press them together, and cut out more scones. Brush the tops gently with cream.

Bake until the scones are golden brown, 15–17 minutes. Transfer the scones to a wire rack and let cool for about 15 minutes.

Serve with the strawberry jam.

hot cross buns

Sweet, spiced hot cross buns are a hallmark of Easter. Flavored with cinnamon, nutmeg, and ginger, they smell incredible while they are baking. If you prefer a traditional paste cross, mix equal parts flour and water to create a paste, and pipe the paste in a cross shape on each bun before baking.

3½ cups (15 oz/450 g) all-purpose flour, plus more as needed

¼ cup (1¾ oz/50 g) sugar

½ teaspoon ground cinnamon

½ teaspoon ground nutmeg

¼ teaspoon ground ginger

½ teaspoon salt

¼ cup (2 oz/60 g) unsalted butter

1¼ cups (310 ml) whole milk

1 package (2¼ teaspoons) active dry yeast

2 large eggs

½ teaspoon grated lemon zest

½ teaspoon grated orange zest

½ cup (3 oz/85 g) packed dried currants or raisins

½ cup (3 oz/90 g) diced mixed candied orange and lemon peel

1 recipe Vanilla Icing (page 170)

MAKES 12 BUNS

In a large bowl, whisk together the flour, sugar, cinnamon, nutmeg, ginger, and salt. Make a well in the center.

In a small saucepan over medium heat, melt the butter, then add the milk. Warm until the mixture is lukewarm (110°F/43°C); if it gets too hot, let it cool slightly. Remove from the heat and whisk in the yeast. Let stand until the yeast is foamy, about 5 minutes, then whisk in 1 egg and the citrus zests until well mixed. Pour the yeast mixture into the well in the flour mixture and stir together with a wooden spoon until a shaggy dough forms.

On a lightly floured work surface, knead the dough until smooth, soft, and elastic, about 10 minutes, dusting with flour as needed to prevent sticking. Press the dough flat and scatter the currants and candied peel evenly on top. Roll up the dough to enclose the fruits, then knead gently to distribute the fruits evenly. Transfer the dough to a large, lightly oiled bowl and cover with plastic wrap or a damp kitchen towel. Set the bowl in a warm spot and let the dough rise until doubled in size, about 1 hour.

Line a baking sheet with parchment paper.

Divide the dough into 12 equal pieces (a kitchen scale works well here), and shape each into a ball. Place them on the prepared baking sheet so they are close but not touching, and cover with a damp kitchen towel. Let rise until doubled in size, 30–60 minutes.

Preheat the oven to 375°F (190°C). Whisk the remaining egg with 1 tablespoon water. Gently brush the buns with the egg wash. Bake until golden brown, 15–18 minutes. Transfer the pan to a wire rack and let cool completely.

Prepare the icing so that you have a smooth but thick icing. Spoon the icing into a 1-qt (1-L) resealable bag and snip a corner off. Use the bag as a piping bag to pipe the icing over the tops of the cooled buns in the shape of a cross. Serve.

rose & vanilla bean tea cakes

This versatile double-vanilla cake makes excellent individual tea cakes, or it can be used as a sheet cake for a crowd. The addition of buttermilk gives the cake a nice tangy richness. A delicately scented rose-vanilla buttercream and a decoration of fresh edible flowers or sugared rose petals adds a sophisticated note.

FOR THE VANILLA
BEAN CAKE

2¾ cups (12 oz/360 g)
all-purpose flour, plus
more for dusting

2½ teaspoons baking powder

¾ teaspoon baking soda

½ teaspoon salt

3 large egg whites
plus 1 large whole egg

2 cups (14 oz/400 g) sugar

¾ cup (6 oz/170 g)
unsalted butter, at cool
room temperature,
plus more for greasing

1 tablespoon vanilla extract

1 vanilla bean, split, with
seeds scraped and reserved

1½ cups (375 ml) buttermilk

FOR DECORATING
1 recipe Quick Vanilla
Buttercream (page 174)

1 tablespoon rose water or
½ teaspoon rose extract

2 drops red food coloring,
plus more as needed (optional)

Fresh, dried, or sugared rose
petals, for garnish

MAKES 12 SMALL CAKES

Preheat the oven to 350°F (180°C). Grease a rimmed 9-by-13-inch (23-by-33-cm) sheet cake pan, line the bottom of the pan with parchment paper, then grease the parchment. Dust with flour, then tap out any excess.

To make the cake, in a bowl, sift together the flour, baking powder, baking soda, and salt. Set aside. In a bowl, using an electric mixer on medium-high speed, beat together the egg whites and 1 cup (7 oz/200 g) of the sugar until soft peaks form, about 4 minutes. Set aside.

In another bowl, using an electric mixer on medium speed, beat together the butter and the remaining 1 cup (7 oz/200 g) sugar until light and fluffy, about 2 minutes. Add the whole egg, vanilla extract, and vanilla bean seeds and beat until combined, about 1 minute. Stop the mixer and scrape down the sides of the bowl. With the mixer on low speed, add the flour mixture in 3 additions, alternating with the buttermilk and beginning and ending with the flour, and beat until combined. Stop the mixer and scrape down the sides of the bowl. Raise the speed to high and beat for 20 seconds.

Using a rubber spatula, gently fold in the egg white mixture until completely incorporated, taking care not to deflate the peaks. Pour the batter into the prepared pan and spread evenly. Bake until a toothpick inserted into the center of the cake comes out clean, about 25 minutes. Transfer the pan to a wire rack and let cool completely, then invert the cake onto a cutting board or an upside-down baking sheet. Remove the parchment paper. Using a 3-inch (7.5-cm) round cutter, cut out 12 rounds. Set aside.

Make the vanilla buttercream, adding the rose water and food coloring, if using, along with the vanilla extract. Beat until completely incorporated, adding more food coloring as desired.

Spread the top of each tea cake with a ¼-inch (6-mm) layer of the buttercream, using an offset spatula to smooth the sides. Garnish with the rose petals and serve.

rhubarb turnovers

Rhubarb is plentiful in the springtime and makes a tart-sweet filling for these flaky turnovers. Look for thin stalks without bruises or blemishes, and make sure you trim off all the leafy bits, as they are poisonous. For strawberry-rhubarb turnovers, substitute strawberries for half of the rhubarb. The rhubarb filling also makes a great compote for cakes, yogurt, or vanilla ice cream.

8 medium stalks rhubarb, sliced into ½-inch (12-mm) pieces

⅔ cup (4¾ oz/140 g) granulated sugar

All-purpose flour, for dusting

1 lb (500 g) frozen puff pastry, thawed

1 large egg, beaten with 1 tablespoon water

Turbinado sugar, for sprinkling

MAKES 8 TURNOVERS

In a saucepan over medium heat, combine the rhubarb and granulated sugar and bring to a simmer. Cook, stirring occasionally, until the rhubarb releases its juices and becomes tender (but before it completely breaks down), about 3 minutes. Remove from the heat and let cool completely.

Line a baking sheet with parchment paper.

On a lightly floured work surface, roll out the puff pastry to a 24-by-12-inch (60-by-30-cm) rectangle. Cut the rectangle into eight 6-inch (15-cm) squares. (Alternatively, if you have two sheets of puff pastry, roll each sheet into a 12-inch [30-cm] square and cut each square into four 6-inch [15-cm] squares.) Place the squares on the prepared baking sheet and refrigerate for 10 minutes.

Preheat the oven to 400°F (200°C). Remove the chilled pastry squares from the refrigerator. Place a scant ¼ cup (1 oz/30 g) rhubarb filling in the center of each square. Brush 2 connecting sides of the dough with a thin layer of egg wash and fold the dough over to make a triangle. Crimp the edges with a fork. Arrange the turnovers on the prepared baking sheet so they are not touching and refrigerate for 10 minutes.

Lightly brush the turnovers with some more of the egg wash, sprinkle with turbinado sugar, and pierce the tops a few times with a fork. Bake until brown and puffy, 20–30 minutes, rotating the baking sheet about halfway through. Let cool slightly, then serve while still warm.

beignets

These pillowy doughnuts, showered with confectioners' sugar, are a favorite treat in New Orleans and would be a welcome addition to any Mardi Gras celebration or festive brunch. Serve them warm out of the fryer with a steaming cup of New Orleans–style chicory coffee for the adults and hot chocolate for the kids.

1 package (2¼ teaspoons) active dry yeast

¼ cup (60 ml) warm water (110°F/43°C)

4½ cups (19 oz/540 g) all-purpose flour, plus more for dusting

3 tablespoons granulated sugar

1 teaspoon salt

¼ cup (2 oz/60 g) unsalted butter

1 cup (250 ml) whole milk

1 large egg

Peanut or canola oil for deep-frying

Confectioners' sugar, for dusting

MAKES ABOUT 12 BEIGNETS

In a small bowl, sprinkle the yeast over the warm water and let stand until a creamy foam forms, 5–10 minutes. In a food processor, combine 3 cups (12¾ oz/360 g) of the flour, the granulated sugar, and salt and process briefly to mix.

In a small saucepan over medium heat, melt the butter then add the milk and heat gently until warm but not steaming. Remove from the heat. With the processor running, pour the milk mixture through the feed tube and process until blended. Add the egg, yeast mixture, and the remaining 1½ cups (6⅓ oz/180 g) flour and process just until a soft dough forms. Oil a large bowl, transfer the dough to it, cover the bowl with plastic wrap, and let the dough rise in a warm, draft-free spot until doubled in size, about 1 hour.

Preheat the oven to 200°F (95°C). Line a baking sheet with paper towels. Pour oil to a depth of 3 inches (7.5 cm) into a deep, heavy saucepan and heat to 360°F (182°C) on a deep-frying thermometer.

While the oil is heating, divide the dough in half. On a lightly floured surface, roll out one half of the dough into a rectangle about ¼ inch (6 mm) thick. Cut into 6 equal rectangles.

When the oil is ready, drop 2 or 3 rectangles into the oil and fry, turning once, until puffed and brown, about 2 minutes on each side. Using a wire skimmer or slotted spoon, transfer to the towel-lined baking sheet and keep warm in the oven. Repeat with the remaining rectangles and then with the remaining dough.

Arrange the beignets on a warmed plate and, using a fine-mesh sieve, dust them heavily all over with confectioners' sugar. Serve at once.

cherry clafoutis

Clafoutis is a French-style baked custard studded with fruit, most often sweet cherries. Make and serve it in a baking dish, or use a 9-inch (23-cm) cast-iron pan for a more rustic touch. A light dusting of confectioners' sugar is all you need for a simple presentation, but dollops of lightly whipped cream would also be a great garnish.

1 lb (500 g) fresh dark sweet cherries, pitted

1 cup (250 ml) whole milk

¼ cup (60 ml) heavy cream

½ cup (2 oz/60 g) cake flour, sifted

4 large eggs, at room temperature

½ cup (3½ oz/100 g) granulated sugar

⅛ teaspoon salt

½ teaspoon almond extract

Confectioners' sugar, for dusting

MAKES 6 SERVINGS

Place a rack in the upper third of the oven and preheat to 350°F (180°C). Generously grease a shallow 1½-qt (1.4-L) baking dish.

Arrange the cherries in the prepared baking dish.

In a saucepan over medium-low heat, warm the milk and cream until small bubbles form around the edges. Remove from the heat and vigorously whisk in the flour, a little at a time, until no lumps remain.

In a bowl, whisk together the eggs, granulated sugar, and salt. Slowly whisk in the milk mixture and the almond extract to make a batter. Pour the batter over the cherries.

Place the dish on a baking sheet and bake until puffed and lightly browned, 45–55 minutes. Let cool on a wire rack for about 10 minutes. Dust with confectioners' sugar and serve warm.

apricot mascarpone crostata

Fragrant apricots are best enjoyed at peak season in late spring and early summer, and this tart is the ideal way to showcase the ripe fruit. The tender almond crust is precooked on the stovetop, then pressed into a pan, so you never have to even turn on the oven—perfect for a hot day. A rich layer of creamy cheese filling lies beneath thinly sliced apricots and a sprinkling of toasted almonds.

FOR THE ALMOND
CROSTATA CRUST

½ cup (2 oz/60 g)
slivered almonds

½ cup (4 oz/115 g)
unsalted butter

1 cup (4¼ oz/120 g)
all-purpose flour

¼ cup (1¾ oz/50 g) sugar

FOR THE APRICOT
MASCARPONE FILLING

6 oz (170 g) cream
cheese, softened

1 cup (8½ oz/240 g)
mascarpone

¼ cup (2 oz/60 g)
crème fraîche

¼ cup (1¾ oz/50 g) sugar

¼ teaspoon almond extract

8 apricots, pitted and
thinly sliced

½ cup (5 oz/140 g)
apricot jam

¼ cup (1 oz/30 g) slivered
almonds, toasted (page 74)

MAKES 6–8 SERVINGS

To make the crust, in a food processor, finely chop the almonds until they resemble coarse bread crumbs.

In a large frying pan over medium-high heat, melt the butter. When it foams, add the flour, sugar, and chopped almonds and cook, stirring occasionally, until the mixture is lightly golden and crumbly, 3–4 minutes. Remove from the heat and let the mixture cool until it can be handled. Press the cooled mixture firmly into the bottom and up the sides of a 9½-inch (24-cm) tart pan with a removable bottom. Refrigerate until chilled, at least 2 hours.

To make the filling, in a bowl, using an electric mixer on medium-high speed, beat the cream cheese, mascarpone, crème fraîche, sugar, and almond extract until smooth. Scrape the filling into the chilled crust. Cover and refrigerate overnight to set the filling.

To serve, remove the tart from the pan and place on a plate. Arrange the apricot slices, slightly overlapping, in concentric circles over the filling. In a small saucepan over low heat, warm the apricot jam until it liquefies, then push the jam through a fine-mesh sieve set over a small bowl to strain out any fruit chunks. Using a pastry brush, gently brush the apricot slices with the warm jam to glaze them. Sprinkle with the toasted almonds and serve.

spring strawberry tart with orange cream

This pretty fruit tart makes use of sweet fresh strawberries at their peak in the springtime. Make the dough and line the tart pan up to 1 week in advance, storing it in the freezer until ready to bake. The simple cream cheese layer is packed with orange flavor. Brushing the strawberries with jam just before serving creates a professional finish.

1 recipe Tart Dough (page 167)

½ lb (250 g) cream cheese, at room temperature

¼ cup (1¾ oz/50 g) sugar

1 teaspoon finely grated orange zest

2 teaspoons Cointreau or other orange liqueur or vanilla extract

2 cups (4 oz/170 g) fresh strawberries, hulled and halved lengthwise

½ cup (5 oz/140 g) apricot jam

MAKES 8 SERVINGS

Prepare the dough and chill as directed. On a lightly floured work surface, roll the dough into a round at least 12 inches (30 cm) in diameter and about ⅛ inch (3 mm) thick. Transfer to a 9½-inch (24-cm) tart pan with a removable bottom and ease into the pan, patting it firmly into the bottom and up the sides of the pan. Trim off any excess dough by running a rolling pin across the top of the pan. Press the dough into the sides to extend it slightly above the rim. Prick the bottom of the tart shell with a fork. Refrigerate or freeze until firm, about 30 minutes.

Position a rack in the lower third of the oven and preheat to 375°F (190°C). Line the tart shell with foil or parchment paper and fill with pie weights or dried beans. Bake until the dough starts to look dry, about 15 minutes. Remove the foil and weights and continue to bake until the crust is golden brown, about 10 minutes longer. Transfer to a wire rack and let cool completely.

In a bowl, using an electric mixer on medium speed, beat together the cream cheese and sugar until smooth. Mix in the orange zest and Cointreau. Spread the cream cheese mixture evenly over the bottom of the tart shell. Arrange the strawberry halves, overlapping them, in concentric circles on top of the cream cheese mixture, completely covering the surface of the tart.

In a small saucepan over low heat, warm the apricot jam until it liquefies. Push through a fine-mesh sieve set over a small bowl to strain out any fruit chunks. Using a pastry brush, gently brush the strawberries with a thin coating of the jam to glaze the fruit. Refrigerate until ready to serve; let sit at room temperature for 20 minutes before serving.

strawberry-rhubarb breakfast cake

Fresh rhubarb is abundant in markets in late spring and early summer, but it can be found year-round in some regions. Although the tart plant is technically a vegetable, it is cooked and sweetened like a fruit. It pairs beautifully with strawberries, such as in this breakfast cake, which would also be welcome for an afternoon tea party.

1⅓ cups (9½ oz/270 g) sugar, plus 2 tablespoons

1½ teaspoons ground cinnamon

4 large eggs

¾ cup (180 ml) avocado or canola oil

2 teaspoons vanilla extract

3 cups (12 oz/345 g) all-purpose flour

2 teaspoons baking powder

½ teaspoon baking soda

1 teaspoon salt

2 pints (1 lb/500 g) fresh strawberries, hulled and coarsely chopped

4 oz (115 g) fresh rhubarb, trimmed and cut crosswise into ½-inch (12-mm) slices

MAKES 8–10 SERVINGS

Preheat the oven to 350°F (180°C). Grease a 9-inch (23-cm) tube pan with removable bottom. In a small bowl, stir together the 2 tablespoons sugar and ½ teaspoon of the cinnamon. Set aside.

In a large bowl, using an electric mixer on medium-high speed, beat the eggs and the 1⅓ cups (9½ oz/270 g) sugar for about 1 minute. Add the oil and vanilla and beat on high speed until thick and pale, about 2 minutes.

In another bowl, whisk together the flour, baking powder, baking soda, remaining 1 teaspoon cinnamon, and salt. Add the flour mixture to the egg mixture and, using the mixer on low speed, beat until thoroughly blended, about 1 minute. Using a rubber spatula, gently fold in the strawberries and rhubarb just until evenly distributed. Do not overmix. Spoon the batter into the prepared pan and spread evenly. Sprinkle evenly with the cinnamon-sugar.

Bake until the topping is golden brown, 60–70 minutes. A toothpick inserted into the center of the cake should come out clean. Run a knife between the cake and the sides of the pan and lift up the center tube to separate the cake from the pan sides. Place on a wire rack to cool completely. Run a knife under the bottom and around the sides of the tube, invert the cake to remove the tube, then place the cake upright on a serving plate. Cut into wedges and serve.

sour cherry pot pies

Fresh sour cherries are only in season for a short stint in late spring and early summer, but they are worth seeking out for their intense tart flavor. If you can't find fresh sour cherries, use frozen or jarred fruits. Be sure to defrost if frozen and drain if jarred. These individual pot pies are ideal for a small gathering, including special occasions. Serve them as is or with a scoop of vanilla ice cream.

1 lb (500 g) frozen puff pastry, thawed

4 cups (10 oz/315 g) pitted sour cherries

¾ cup (5 oz/140 g) sugar

¼ cup (1 oz/30 g) all-purpose flour, plus more for dusting

1 tablespoon fresh lemon juice

2 tablespoons unsalted butter, cut into pieces

1 large egg, lightly beaten with 1 teaspoon warm water

MAKES 6 POT PIES

Have ready six 6-ounce (180-ml) ramekins. Line a baking sheet with parchment paper.

On a floured work surface, roll out the pastry ⅛ inch (3 mm) thick. Cut out 6 circles from the dough with the same circumference as the ramekins. Transfer the pastry circles to the prepared baking sheet and prick them all over with a fork. Cover with plastic wrap and refrigerate for 30 minutes.

Meanwhile, preheat the oven to 375°F (190°C). In a saucepan over medium-high heat, stir together the cherries, sugar, flour, and lemon juice and cook, stirring occasionally, until thickened, about 10 minutes. Remove from the heat, stir in the butter, and divide the filling among the prepared ramekins. Set aside.

Brush the pastry circles with the egg wash. Bake until very lightly golden and puffed, about 12 minutes. Carefully transfer the pastries to the ramekins, covering the cherry filling and pressing down lightly. Place the ramekins on the baking sheet.

Bake until the filling is bubbling and the pastry is crisp and golden brown, about 30 minutes. Let cool slightly before serving.

mini red velvet cupcakes with cream cheese frosting

With a velvety red crumb, delicate cocoa flavor, and cream cheese frosting, red velvet cupcakes are arguably one of the most popular cupcake flavors. Cake flour is a fine-textured, soft wheat flour that helps make cakes and pastries tender and not chewy.

1¼ cups (5½ oz/150 g) cake flour

2 tablespoons unsweetened cocoa powder

¾ teaspoon baking powder

¼ teaspoon salt

½ cup (125 ml) buttermilk

1 teaspoon vanilla extract

½ teaspoon white vinegar

4 drops red gel food coloring

¾ cup (5 oz/140 g) sugar

¼ cup (2 oz/60 g) unsalted butter, at cool room temperature

1 large egg, at room temperature

1 recipe Cream Cheese Frosting (page 173)

MAKES 24 MINI CUPCAKES

Preheat the oven to 350°F (180°C). Line 24 mini muffin cups with paper liners.

In a bowl, sift together the cake flour, cocoa powder, baking powder, and salt. In a small bowl, whisk together the buttermilk, vanilla, vinegar, and food coloring. In another bowl, using an electric mixer on medium-high speed, beat the sugar and butter until pale and creamy, about 2 minutes. Beat in the egg. Reduce the speed to low and add the flour mixture in 3 additions, alternating with the buttermilk mixture and beginning and ending with the flour, and beat until combined, scraping down the sides of the bowl as needed.

Divide the batter among the prepared muffin cups, filling them about three-fourths full. Bake until a toothpick inserted into the center of a cupcake comes out clean, about 15 minutes. Transfer the pan to a wire rack and let the cupcakes cool in the pan for about 5 minutes. Remove the cupcakes from the pans and let cool completely on the rack, about 30 minutes.

While the cupcakes cool, make the frosting. Transfer the frosting to a pastry bag fitted with a ½-inch (12-mm) star tip, then pipe the frosting decoratively onto each cupcake. Serve.

strawberry cheesecake cupcakes

Sticky-sweet strawberry jam is swirled into these muffin-size cheesecakes to create a pretty effect. They are great for a party, because you can make them a day in advance. Experiment with other flavors of berry jam, like blackberry or raspberry, to mix it up.

FOR THE CRUST

⅔ cup (2 oz/80 g) graham cracker crumbs (about 6 crackers), broken into pieces

2 teaspoons sugar

3 tablespoons unsalted butter, melted

Pinch of salt

FOR THE FILLING

½ cup (5 oz/140 g) strawberry jam, store-bought or homemade (page 25)

Fresh lemon juice, as needed (optional)

1 lb (500 g) cream cheese, at room temperature

⅔ cup (4¾ oz/140 g) sugar

¼ cup (2 oz/55 g) sour cream

1 teaspoon vanilla extract

2 large eggs

1 tablespoon all-purpose flour

MAKES 16 CUPCAKES

Preheat the oven to 325°F (165°C). Line 16 standard muffin cups with paper liners.

To make the crust, in a food processor, process the graham crackers to fine crumbs. Pour the crumbs into a bowl. Add the sugar, butter, and salt and, using a fork, stir until the crumbs are evenly moistened. Divide the mixture evenly among the prepared muffin cups (about 1 tablespoon per cup). Press the crumbs into the bottom of each cup. Bake until lightly golden, about 4 minutes. Transfer the pans to a wire rack and let cool.

To make the filling, in a clean food processor bowl, process the jam until smooth. If the jam is very thick, add a little lemon juice or water to thin it until it is like a sauce. Scrape into a bowl and set aside. Clean the processor bowl.

In the food processor, process the cream cheese until smooth, about 3 minutes. Add the sugar and process until smooth, about 30 seconds. Scrape down the sides of the bowl. Add the sour cream and vanilla and process until combined. Add the eggs one at a time, processing well after each addition. Add the flour and process until combined. Scrape down the sides of the bowl, then process until smooth and combined.

Divide the filling evenly among the prepared muffin cups, filling each three-fourths full. Top each with a small amount of the jam, then use a toothpick to swirl the mixtures together, creating a marbled look. Bake until the cheesecakes puff and are set, about 23 minutes. Transfer the pans to wire racks and let cool completely. Cover with plastic wrap and refrigerate until chilled, at least 3 hours or up to overnight. Serve.

crème brûlée tartlets

Here, creamy vanilla bean custard is encased in a thin layer of pastry, then topped with a crunchy sugar crust. A timeless showstopper, the tartlets can be made in advance and then you only need to caramelize the sugary tops right before serving.

1 recipe Tart Dough
(page 167)

2 cups (500 ml) heavy cream

½ vanilla bean, split lengthwise

2 large eggs, plus 2 large
egg yolks

⅓ cup (2½ oz/70 g)
granulated sugar

⅛ teaspoon salt

¼ cup (1¾ oz/50 g)
turbinado sugar, finely
ground in a food processor

**MAKES SIX 4-INCH/10-CM
TARTLETS**

Prepare the dough and chill as directed. On a lightly floured work surface, roll the dough into a round at least 12 inches (30 cm) in diameter and about ⅛ inch (3 mm) thick. Using a 6-inch (15-cm) plate and a small, sharp knife, cut out 3 or 4 rounds from the tart dough. Press the dough scraps together and reroll to cut out additional rounds. You should have a total of 6 rounds.

Transfer the rounds to six 4-inch (10-cm) tartlet pans with removable bottoms. Ease into the pans and pat firmly into the bottoms and up the sides. Trim off any excess dough. Press the dough in the sides to extend it slightly above the rims. Prick the bottom of the tartlet shells with a fork. Refrigerate or freeze until firm, about 30 minutes.

Position an oven rack in the lower third of the oven and preheat to 375°F (190°C). Place the tartlet shells on a baking sheet. Line each with foil or parchment paper and fill with pie weights or dried beans. Bake until the dough starts to look dry, about 15 minutes. Remove the foil and weights and continue to bake until the crust is golden brown, about 5 minutes longer. Transfer to a wire rack and let cool completely.

In a saucepan over medium heat, warm the cream until hot and steaming. Scrape the seeds from the vanilla bean into the cream, then add the pod. In a bowl, whisk together the eggs, egg yolks, granulated sugar, and salt until pale yellow. Slowly add 1 cup (250 ml) of the hot cream while whisking constantly. Whisk in the remaining cream. Return the mixture to the saucepan over medium heat and cook, whisking constantly, until the custard is thick enough to heavily coat the back of a spoon, 4–5 minutes. Strain through a medium-mesh sieve placed over a measuring pitcher. Pour into the tart shells, dividing evenly. Refrigerate until well chilled, 3–4 hours.

To serve, position a rack 3–4 inches (7.5–10 cm) below the broiler and preheat the broiler; alternatively, have ready a kitchen torch. Sprinkle each tartlet with 2 teaspoons of the turbinado sugar. Broil or blowtorch the tartlets until the sugar caramelizes, 1–2 minutes. Transfer to a wire rack and let cool for 10 minutes. Remove the tart pan sides from each tart, then slide the tartlets onto individual plates. Serve at once.

coconut lime curd layer cake

This magnificently tall 3-layer buttermilk cake is filled with zesty lime curd and coated in coconut buttercream. Try spreading the buttercream thinly around the sides of the cake for a "naked cake" effect, which is gorgeous when topped with colorful edible flowers and a sprinkle of finely grated lime zest. If you like, divide the batter between two 9-inch (23-cm) cake pans, then split the layers for a 4-layer cake.

1 recipe Lime Curd
(page 177)

1 recipe Coconut Buttercream
(page 175)

FOR THE VANILLA
BUTTERMILK CAKE

4 cups (17 oz/510 g) plus
2 tablespoons all-purpose flour

3¾ teaspoons baking powder

1⅛ teaspoons baking soda

1 teaspoon salt

4 large egg whites,
plus 2 large eggs

3 cups (21 oz/600 g) sugar

1 cup (8 oz/225 g) plus
2 tablespoons unsalted butter,
at cool room temperature,
plus more for greasing

2¼ cups (560 ml) buttermilk

1½ tablespoons vanilla extract

Edible flowers and grated
lime zest, for garnish

MAKES 12–18 SERVINGS

Make the lime curd and coconut buttercream. Cover and refrigerate until ready to use or for up to 3 days.

To make the cake, preheat the oven to 350°F (180°C). Grease three 8-inch (20-cm) round cake pans, line the bottoms of the pans with parchment paper, then grease the parchment. Dust with flour, then tap out any excess.

In a bowl, sift together the flour, baking powder, baking soda, and salt. Set aside.

In a bowl, using an electric mixer on medium-high speed, beat together the egg whites and 1 cup (7 oz/200g) of the sugar until soft peaks form, about 5 minutes. Set aside.

In another bowl, using the electric mixer on medium speed, beat together the butter and the remaining 2 cups (14 oz/400 g) sugar until light and fluffy, about 2 minutes. Add the eggs one at a time and beat until incorporated, about 1 minute. Stop the mixer and scrape down the sides of the bowl. With the mixer on low speed, add the flour mixture in 3 additions, alternating with the buttermilk and beginning and ending with the flour, and beat until combined. Beat in the vanilla. Stop the mixer and scrape down the sides of the bowl. Raise the speed to high and beat for 20 seconds. Using a rubber spatula, gently fold the egg white mixture into the batter until completely incorporated, taking care not to deflate the peaks.

Divide the batter evenly among the prepared pans and spread evenly. Bake until a toothpick inserted into the center of the cakes comes out clean, 40–45 minutes. Transfer the pans to wire racks and let cool for 10 minutes, then invert the cakes onto the racks and let cool completely.

Transfer one-fourth of the buttercream to a pastry bag fitted with a ½-inch (12-mm) round tip.

To assemble the cake, place 1 cake layer, top side up, on a cake stand or serving plate. Pipe a ring of buttercream around the edge of the cake, then fill the center with half of the lime curd. Top with a second cake layer, pipe a ring of buttercream, and fill the center with the remaining lime curd. Top with the third cake layer and spread the remaining buttercream over the top. If desired, reserve a small amount of buttercream and spread a thin layer on the sides to create a "naked" cake effect.

Garnish the cake with edible flowers and lime zest and serve.

passion fruit cupcakes with coconut frosting

Tropical passion fruit has a tart-sweet flavor and a floral, citrus fragrance that pairs beautifully with vanilla and coconut. Here, the pulp is transformed into a silky curd that fills vanilla-scented cupcakes topped with coconut frosting. Fresh passion fruits are available year-round from well-stocked grocers, but the pulp can also be found in the freezer section.

FOR THE
PASSION FRUIT CURD

4 ripe passion fruits, or
¼ cup (60 ml) thawed frozen
passion fruit pulp (seedless)

2 large egg yolks

⅓ cup (2½ oz/70 g)
granulated sugar

Pinch of salt

3 tablespoons unsalted butter,
cut into pieces

FOR THE CUPCAKES

1¾ cups (7½ oz/210 g)
all-purpose flour

2 teaspoons baking powder

¼ teaspoon salt

¾ cup (6 oz/170 g) unsalted
butter, at cool room temperature

⅔ cup (4¾ oz/140 g)
granulated sugar

2 large eggs

1 cup (250 ml) heavy cream

1 teaspoon vanilla extract

MAKES 12 CUPCAKES

To make the curd, cut the passion fruits in half and scoop the pulp into a fine-mesh sieve set over a bowl. Press on the pulp to push it through the sieve; discard the seeds.

Measure ¼ cup (60 ml) pulp and juice and place in a small saucepan. Whisk in the egg yolks, granulated sugar, and salt. Cook over low heat, whisking constantly, until the mixture thickens and turns a bright orange-yellow (do not let it boil), 2–3 minutes. Remove from the heat and whisk in the butter. Strain the mixture through a fine-mesh sieve into a bowl. Let cool for 15 minutes. Press plastic wrap directly onto the surface of the curd and refrigerate until chilled, about 2 hours.

To make the cupcakes, preheat the oven to 375°F (190°C). Line 12 standard muffin cups with paper liners.

In a bowl, sift together the flour, baking powder, and salt.

In a large bowl, using an electric mixer on low speed, beat the butter and sugar until blended, then raise the speed to medium-high and beat until light and fluffy, 1–2 minutes. Add the eggs one at a time and beat until incorporated. Reduce the speed to low and add the dry ingredients in 3 additions, alternating with the cream, beginning and ending with the dry ingredients. Beat in the vanilla. Divide the batter among the prepared muffin cups, filling them nearly full. Bake until a toothpick inserted into the center of a cupcake comes out clean, about 20 minutes. Let the cupcakes cool in the pan for 10 minutes. Remove the cupcakes from the pan and let cool completely on the rack.

continued on page 46

continued from page 44

FOR THE
COCONUT FROSTING

½ cup (2 oz/60 g) sweetened shredded dried coconut

½ cup (4 oz/115 g) unsalted butter, at cool room temperature

3¾ cups (15 oz/435 g) confectioners' sugar

⅓ cup (80 ml) coconut milk

Edible flowers, for garnish

To make the coconut frosting, reduce the oven temperature to 325°F (165°C). Spread the coconut in a single layer on a baking sheet and toast, stirring occasionally, until fragrant and lightly golden, about 5 minutes. Let cool completely.

In a bowl, using an electric mixer on medium-low speed, beat the butter with half of the confectioners' sugar until crumbly. Add the remaining confectioners' sugar and beat about 1 minute. With the mixer on medium speed, slowly add the coconut milk and beat until blended. Raise the speed to medium-high and beat the frosting until light and fluffy, about 1 minute.

Using a paring knife, cut a cone-shaped core about 1½ inches (4 cm) wide halfway down into the center of each cupcake. Gently remove the cores and set aside. Fill each cupcake with about 1 tablespoon of the curd. Trim the bottom off the cores and replace the tops of the cores. Spread the frosting over the top of the cupcakes and sprinkle with the toasted coconut. Let the frosting set for about 15 minutes. Garnish with edible flowers and serve.

orange vanilla bean sponge cake with sugared strawberries

This light orange-and-vanilla-scented tube cake is made with Passover cake meal, a fine matzo meal specifically formulated for cake baking. Look for it in kosher markets or well-stocked food stores. Topped with spring-fresh sugared strawberries tossed with another hit of orange zest, this is a simple yet delightful end to a holiday meal.

FOR THE ORANGE
SPONGE CAKE

1½ cups (10½ oz/300 g) sugar

1 vanilla bean, split lengthwise
and seeds scraped

10 large eggs, separated,
at room temperature

½ cup (125 ml) fresh
orange juice

1 tablespoon finely grated
orange zest

¼ teaspoon salt

¾ cup (4 oz/120 g)
Passover cake meal

½ cup (2½ oz/75 g)
potato starch

FOR THE SUGARED
STRAWBERRIES

2 pints (1 lb/500 g) fresh
strawberries, hulled and sliced

3 tablespoons sugar,
or to taste

1 teaspoon finely grated
orange zest

MAKES 8 SERVINGS

Preheat the oven to 325°F (165°C). In a food processor, combine the sugar and vanilla bean seeds and process until finely ground. Set aside.

To make the cake, in a bowl, using an electric mixer set on high speed, beat the egg yolks until very thick and pale, about 4 minutes. Place the vanilla sugar in a sifter and sift directly onto the yolks. Continue to beat until the mixture is thick and pale and tripled in volume, about 5 minutes. Gradually beat in the orange juice and zest.

In a clean bowl, using clean, dry beaters, beat the egg whites and salt until stiff but not dry. Set aside. Combine the cake meal and potato starch in the sifter and sift the mixture directly onto the egg yolk mixture. Using a rubber spatula, fold in gently but thoroughly. Then fold in the egg white mixture, again working gently but thoroughly.

Pour the batter into a 12-cup (680-g) tube pan or angel food cake pan. Bake until golden and the top of the cake springs back when gently touched, about 50 minutes. Invert the cake in its pan onto the neck of a bottle. Let cool completely.

To make the strawberries, about 15 minutes before serving, in a bowl, stir together the strawberries, sugar, and orange zest. Taste and add more sugar if you like.

To remove the cake from the pan, run a sharp knife around the edge of the pan to loosen the cake, then invert the cake onto a cake plate. Carefully lift off the pan. Serve slices topped with the sugared strawberries and their juices.

bittersweet chocolate almond torte

This simple gluten-free cake relies on only a few ingredients to make it great. Be sure to use the good-quality chocolate and fresh almonds for the best flavor. A light dusting of confectioners' sugar and some fresh fruit or a dollop of whipped cream are all it needs to shine. You can also use all semisweet or all bittersweet chocolate in the recipe.

½ cup (2 oz/60 g) slivered almonds

½ cup (3½ oz/100 g) granulated sugar

5 oz (140 g) semisweet chocolate, finely chopped

5 oz (140 g) bittersweet chocolate, finely chopped

½ cup (4 oz/115 g) unsalted butter, plus more for greasing

8 large eggs, separated

Confectioners' sugar, for dusting

1 recipe Whipped Cream (page 176), for serving (optional)

MAKES 6–8 SERVINGS

Preheat the oven to 300°F (150°C). Grease the bottom and sides of a 9-inch (23-cm) springform pan. Line the bottom with a round of parchment paper.

In a food processor, process the almonds and granulated sugar until powdery. Set aside.

Place the chocolates and butter in a heatproof bowl set over but not touching barely simmering water in a saucepan, or in the top of a double boiler, and heat, stirring often, until the chocolate and butter melt. Remove from the heat. In a bowl, whisk together the egg yolks, then whisk in a little of the chocolate mixture. Pour the egg yolk mixture back into the bowl with the chocolate mixture and whisk until combined.

In another bowl, using an electric mixer on medium-high speed, beat the egg whites until medium peaks form. Stir one-fourth of the whites into the chocolate mixture. Using a rubber spatula, gently fold in the ground almond mixture. Gently and thoroughly fold in the remaining egg whites. Scrape the batter into the prepared pan.

Bake until the cake puffs up a little and jiggles very slightly when gently shaken, 30–35 minutes. If the center looks soupy, bake for another 5 minutes. Let cool in the pan on a wire rack for 10 minutes, then remove the pan sides. Cover the cake with a clean, slightly damp kitchen towel so that the outside does not dry out. Let cool completely on the rack.

To serve, dust the cooled cake with confectioners' sugar. Serve with whipped cream, if you like.

angel food cake
with strawberry-rhubarb compote

Angel food cake relies on stiffly beaten egg whites to achieve its lofty heights. The result is a light, airy cake with a distinctive texture that is ideal for pairing with fruit compotes and whipped cream. This springtime strawberry-rhubarb compote has a hint of orange. Any leftover compote is equally delicious served over ice cream or vanilla yogurt.

FOR THE
ANGEL FOOD CAKE

1 cup (4¼ oz/120 g) cake flour

1¾ cups (12 oz/340 g) sugar

12 large egg whites,
at room temperature

1 teaspoon cream of tartar

¼ teaspoon salt

2 teaspoons vanilla extract

½ teaspoon almond extract

MAKES 10–12 SERVINGS

To make the cake, place a rack in the lower third of the oven and preheat to 325°F (165°C). In a small bowl, sift together the flour and ¾ cup (5 oz/140 g) of the sugar. Set aside.

In a large bowl, using an electric mixer on medium speed, beat together the egg whites, cream of tartar, and salt until foamy, about 2 minutes. Raise the speed to medium-high and continue to beat while slowly adding the remaining 1 cup (7 oz/200 g) sugar, until soft, glossy peaks form, 2–3 minutes. Continue to beat until medium-stiff peaks form, about 2 minutes. Reduce the speed to medium, add the vanilla and almond extracts, and beat until stiff peaks form, about 1 minute; do not overbeat.

Reduce the speed to low, add one-third of the flour mixture, and beat just until well incorporated. Add the remaining flour mixture in 2 batches and beat just until incorporated.

Using a large rubber spatula, scrape the batter into an ungreased 10-inch (25-cm) angel food cake pan, then gently smooth the top of the batter with the spatula.

Bake until the cake springs back when lightly touched, about 40 minutes. If firm, insert a toothpick near the center of the cake. If it comes out dry, the cake is done. If it comes out wet or with crumbs on it, bake for 5 minutes longer and check again. Repeat until the cake is done.

Remove the cake from the oven and invert the cake in the pan onto a work surface. Let cool until the cake and the pan are cool to the touch, about 1 hour.

FOR THE STRAWBERRY-
RHUBARB COMPOTE

¼ cup (60 ml) fresh
orange juice

⅓ cup (2½ oz/70 g) sugar

Pinch of salt

½ lb (225 g) rhubarb, cut
into ¼-inch (6-mm) slices

2 pints (1 lb/500 g)
fresh strawberries,
hulled and quartered

1½ teaspoons cornstarch

1 recipe Whipped Cream
(page 176), for serving

While the cake cools, make the compote. In a saucepan over medium-high heat, combine 3 tablespoons of the orange juice, the sugar, and the salt. Bring to a simmer. Add the rhubarb, bring to a boil, reduce the heat to medium-low, and simmer, stirring occasionally, until softened, about 5 minutes. Add the strawberries and simmer until softened, about 2 minutes.

In a small bowl, mix the cornstarch and the remaining 1 tablespoon orange juice and stir into the rhubarb mixture. Simmer just until thickened. Let cool to room temperature.

To loosen the cake, run a knife around the sides of the pan. Turn the cake out of the pan and place it right side up on a serving plate. Serve wedges topped with the compote and whipped cream.

carrot cake

Baked as a thick single layer and spread with gooey cream cheese frosting, this spiced cake is a perfect addition to a potluck or picnic. To make a layered version, divide the batter between two 9-inch (23-cm) cake pans and decrease the baking time by about 10 minutes. Spread the frosting between layers, then frost the top and sides.

2 cups (9 oz/240 g) cake flour

2 teaspoons baking powder

2 teaspoons baking soda

1 teaspoon ground cinnamon

¼ teaspoon ground nutmeg

½ teaspoon salt

1½ cups (10½ oz/300 g) sugar

4 large eggs

1¼ cups (315 ml) avocado or canola oil

Grated zest of 1 orange

About 3 cups (15 oz/470 g) grated peeled carrots

1 recipe Cream Cheese Frosting (page 173)

MAKES 10–12 SERVINGS

Preheat the oven to 350°F (180°C). Lightly coat a 9-by-13-inch (23-by-33-cm) baking pan with nonstick cooking spray.

Sift the flour, baking powder, baking soda, cinnamon, nutmeg, and salt onto a sheet of parchment paper. In a large bowl, whisk the sugar, eggs, oil, and orange zest until thoroughly combined. Stir in the carrots. Using a rubber spatula, fold in the flour mixture just until incorporated. Pour the batter into the prepared pan.

Bake until a toothpick inserted into the center of the cake comes out clean, 35–40 minutes. Watch closely at the end so that the cake does not overbake. Transfer the pan to a wire rack and let cool for 15 minutes, then invert the cake onto the rack and let cool completely. Cover with a clean, slightly damp kitchen towel so that the exterior of the cake does not dry out.

Transfer the cooled cake to a platter. Using an icing spatula, frost the cake with a thick layer of cream cheese frosting and serve.

king cake

King cake—a sweet, yeasted, ring-shaped bread that is decorated with sparkling sugar stripes of purple, green, and gold—is a staple of Mardi Gras. Often an ovenproof baby-shaped charm is hidden inside the bread, with the lucky recipient promised luck and prosperity for the year to come.

⅓ cup (2½ oz/70 g) sugar

Grated zest of 1 lemon

4 cups (17 oz/510 g) all-purpose flour

1 package (2¼ teaspoons) instant yeast

1 teaspoon salt

¾ cup (6 oz/170 g) cold unsalted butter, cut into small pieces

3 large eggs, at room temperature

1 cup (250 ml) warm whole milk (110°F/43°C)

1 ovenproof charm, such as a Mardi Gras baby, or a whole almond

1 large egg yolk whisked with 1 tablespoon water, for brushing

Purple, green, and gold (or yellow) decorating sugars

MAKES 16 SERVINGS

In a food processor, combine the sugar and lemon zest and process for 15 seconds to mix well. Add the flour, yeast, and salt and process again for 15 seconds to mix well. Scatter the butter pieces evenly over the flour mixture, then push them down into the flour mixture. Pulse about 15 times, until the mixture resembles bread crumbs.

In a large liquid measuring pitcher or a bowl with a spout, whisk together the eggs and milk. With the processor running, pour the egg mixture through the feed tube and process for about 30 seconds, stopping to scrape down the sides of the processor if necessary. The dough should be soft and sticky.

Scrape the dough into a large bowl, cover tightly, and refrigerate overnight. It will stiffen as it chills to the consistency of a dense cookie dough.

Line a baking sheet with parchment paper. Working quickly, before the dough warms up and begins to soften, transfer the cold dough to the parchment and, using your hands, mold it into an oblong ring about 12 inches (30 cm) long and 2 inches (5 cm) wide with a hole in the center. Dampen your hands and pat the ring gently to smooth the surface. Push the charm into the underside of the dough to conceal it. Cover the dough ring loosely with another sheet of parchment. Set the pan in a warm, draft-free place and let the dough rise until doubled in size, about 3 hours.

Preheat the oven to 375°F (190°C). Brush the surface of the dough gently and evenly with the egg yolk mixture. Sprinkle generously with the decorating sugars, alternating wide stripes of purple, green, and gold. Bake the cake until golden brown, 25–30 minutes. Transfer the pan to a wire rack and let cool for at least 10 minutes.

Transfer the cake to a cake plate. Serve warm or at room temperature, cut on the diagonal into thin slices.

summer

blackberry cobbler

There's nothing like coming across a blackberry bush at the peak of summer covered in sweet, juicy berries and picking them to your heart's content. This easy dessert makes use of fresh summer berries, highlighted by tangy lemon zest and topped with fluffy biscuits. Be sure to serve bowls of the warm cobbler with scoops of ice cream.

FOR THE BLACKBERRY FILLING

2 pints (1 lb/450 g) fresh blackberries

¾ cup (5 oz/140 g) sugar

3 tablespoons tapioca starch

Finely grated zest and juice of 1 lemon

FOR THE BISCUIT TOPPING

1 cup (4¼ oz/120 g) all-purpose flour

¼ cup (1¾ oz/50 g) sugar

1 teaspoon baking powder

¼ teaspoon salt

Finely grated zest of 1 lemon

5 tablespoons (2½ oz/75 g) cold unsalted butter, cut into pieces, plus more for greasing

1 large egg

⅓ cup (80 ml) heavy cream

Vanilla ice cream, for serving (optional)

MAKES 8 SERVINGS

Place a rack in the lower third of the oven and preheat to 350°F (180°C). Grease a 2-qt (2-L) baking dish.

To make the filling, in a bowl, combine the blackberries, sugar, tapioca starch, and lemon zest and juice. Stir gently to mix, then pour the filling into the prepared dish and spread evenly.

To make the topping, in a large bowl, stir together the flour, sugar, baking powder, salt, and lemon zest. Using a pastry blender or your fingers, cut in, or rub, the butter into the flour mixture until the texture resembles coarse cornmeal, leaving some pieces of butter about the size of small peas. In a small bowl, beat together the egg and cream, then add to the flour mixture a little at a time and stir just until the mixture comes together.

Pinch off chunks of the topping and place them on top of the blackberry mixture, covering it nearly completely. Bake until the topping is firm and golden brown and the filling bubbles slowly, 45–55 minutes. Let cool for about 45 minutes. Serve with scoops of ice cream, if you like.

lemon crinkle cookies

With a thin, crackly crust coated in confectioners' sugar and a chewy interior, these cookies are sure to become a family favorite. The lemon-sweet flavor is like a burst of summer sunshine. Plan to make the dough at least an hour before baking, or make it up to a day in advance so you are ready to go at a moment's notice.

2 cups (9 oz/240 g) all-purpose flour

2 teaspoons baking powder

¼ teaspoon salt

½ cup (4 oz/115 g) unsalted butter, at cool room temperature

1 cup (7 oz/200 g) granulated sugar

1 tablespoon finely grated lemon zest

3 large eggs

3 tablespoons fresh lemon juice

1 teaspoon vanilla extract

½ cup (2 oz/60 g) confectioners' sugar, sifted

MAKES ABOUT 28 COOKIES

In a bowl, whisk together the flour, baking powder, and salt.

In a large bowl, using an electric mixer on medium speed, beat the butter, granulated sugar, and lemon zest until creamy, about 2 minutes. Add the eggs one at a time, beating well after each addition. Turn off the mixer and scrape down the sides of the bowl. Add the lemon juice and vanilla and beat until blended. Reduce the speed to low, add the flour mixture, and mix just until blended. Cover the bowl with plastic wrap and refrigerate for at least 1 hour or up to overnight.

Place 1 rack in the upper third and 1 rack in the lower third of the oven and preheat to 350°F (180°C). Line 2 baking sheets with parchment paper. Put the confectioners' sugar into a shallow bowl.

Scoop up a rounded tablespoon of the chilled dough and roll it between your palms into a rough ball. Roll the ball in the confectioners' sugar until completely covered and place on a prepared baking sheet. Repeat with the remaining dough, spacing the cookies about 2 inches (5 cm) apart. Flatten each ball slightly with the palm of your hand.

Bake for 7 minutes, then rotate the baking sheets between the two racks. Continue to bake until the cookies are cracked and puffed and the edges are just starting to brown, about 6 minutes longer. Transfer the baking sheets to wire racks and let the cookies cool on the sheets for 5 minutes, then transfer the cookies to the racks and let cool completely.

dulce de leche alfajores

Dulce de leche is a sticky, gooey caramel that is perfect for pressing between two shortbread rounds. Alfajores are a traditional sweet found in most Latin American countries, but they originated in the Middle East. They can be dusted with confectioners' sugar, rolled in toasted coconut, or dipped in melted dark chocolate.

2 cups (9 oz/240 g) all-purpose flour, sifted, plus more for dusting

¼ teaspoon salt

¾ cup (6 oz/170 g) cold unsalted butter, cut into small pieces

¼ cup (1 oz/30 g) confectioners' sugar, plus more for dusting

2 teaspoons vanilla extract

1 cup (11 oz/300 g) store-bought dulce de leche

MAKES ABOUT 16 COOKIES

Preheat the oven to 325°F (165°C). Line 2 baking sheets with parchment paper.

In a food processor, combine the flour and salt and pulse until blended. Add the butter, sugar, and vanilla and pulse until the dough forms a ball and pulls away from the sides of the bowl. Turn the dough out onto a lightly floured work surface and shape into a disk. Roll out the dough to a thickness of ⅛ inch (3 mm).

Using a 2½-inch (6-cm) round cutter, cut out cookies. Gather up the dough scraps, press them together just until smooth, reroll, and cut out additional cookies. You should have at least 32 cookies. (If the dough becomes too soft to handle, place it in the freezer for 2–3 minutes, then finish rolling and cutting.)

Transfer the cookies to the prepared sheets, spacing them about 1½ inches (4 cm) apart. Bake until the surfaces of the cookies are dry to the touch, 10–12 minutes. Transfer the cookies to wire racks and let cool completely.

Carefully spread 1 tablespoon of the dulce de leche on the flat side of half the cookies, being careful not to break the cookies. Place a second cookie, flat side down, on top of the filling and gently press together. Dust the cookies with confectioners' sugar and serve.

lime curd coconut bars

This tropical riff on a classic lemon bar adds sweet coconut and lime zest to the buttery crust, and substitutes lime juice for lemon juice in the curd topping. The sweet-tart bars are a perfect end to a summer BBQ or outdoor event. Be sure to top them with the confectioners' sugar just before serving.

1 cup (8 oz/225 g) unsalted butter, at cool room temperature, plus more for greasing

¼ cup (2 oz/60 g) firmly packed light brown sugar

2 cups (9 oz/240 g) all-purpose flour

Finely grated zest of 1 lime

½ cup (2 oz/60 g) sweetened shredded dried coconut

½ teaspoon salt

1¾ cups (12 oz/340 g) granulated sugar

1 tablespoon cornstarch

1 teaspoon baking powder

4 large eggs, lightly beaten

¾ cup (180 ml) fresh lime juice

Confectioners' sugar, for dusting

MAKES 24 BARS

Preheat the oven to 350°F (180°C). Lightly grease a 9-by-13-inch (23-by-33-cm) baking dish. Line the bottom and sides with parchment paper, letting the paper overhang on opposite sides by 2 inches (5 cm).

In a large bowl, using an electric mixer on medium speed, beat the butter and brown sugar until fluffy, 3–4 minutes. Add the flour, half of the lime zest, the coconut, and half of the salt and mix until the dough just holds together. Gently press the dough into the bottom of the dish and prick it with a fork all over. Bake until golden, about 20 minutes.

In another bowl, whisk together the granulated sugar, cornstarch, baking powder, and remaining lime zest and salt. Whisk in the eggs and lime juice until well combined and smooth. Pour the mixture into the crust and bake for 20–25 minutes.

Transfer the baking dish to a wire rack and let cool, then refrigerate until set, about 2 hours. Use the parchment paper to lift the dessert from the dish. Cut into 24 bars and dust with confectioners' sugar.

plum jam oatmeal streusel bars

A single spiced oat-filled dough is used for both the base and the crumbly topping in these jam-filled bars. Tart-sweet plum jam is the epitome of summer, and if you have fresh plums on hand, they can easily be simmered into homemade preserves. But these bars would be terrific with apricot, nectarine, peach, or raspberry jam too.

1⅔ cups (7¼ oz/200 g) all-purpose flour

1 cup (7½ oz/210 g) firmly packed light brown sugar

Finely grated zest of 1 small orange

1 teaspoon ground cinnamon

¼ teaspoon baking soda

¼ teaspoon salt

2 teaspoons vanilla extract

¾ cup (6 oz/170 g) cold unsalted butter, cut into small pieces

1⅓ cups (5½ oz/170 g) rolled oats

1½ cups (15 oz/420 g) plum jam

MAKES ABOUT 18 BARS

Preheat the oven to 350°F (180°C). Grease a 9-by-13-inch (23-by-33-cm) baking dish with nonstick cooking spray.

In a food processor, combine the flour, sugar, orange zest, cinnamon, baking soda, salt, vanilla, and butter and pulse until the mixture looks like chunky crumbs. Add the oats and pulse a few times to mix.

Transfer two-thirds of the mixture to the prepared dish and press it firmly into an even layer. The dough will be crumbly. Press it down firmly with the bottom of a flat glass. Spread the jam evenly over the top, then sprinkle the remaining oat mixture over the jam.

Bake until the top is golden brown and the jam is bubbling, 35–40 minutes. Let cool in the dish, then cut into bars.

caramel orange flan

Silky flan makes the perfect ending to any Mexican-inspired meal. When turned out onto a serving plate, the caramel forms a rich, flavorful sauce. Be sure to cook the caramel until it's deeply golden browned, but take it off the heat before it burns. Work quickly to ensure you coat the entire dish with the melted caramel before it hardens.

1¾ cups (12 oz/340 g) sugar

1 teaspoon light corn syrup

2 cups (500 ml) whole milk

1 cup (250 ml) half-and-half

1 teaspoon finely grated orange zest

Pinch of salt

4 large eggs

1 teaspoon vanilla extract

MAKES ONE 9-INCH (23-CM) FLAN

Have ready a deep 9-inch (23-cm) ceramic or glass pie dish and a large shallow baking pan that will hold the dish.

In a saucepan over medium heat, combine 1 cup (7 oz/200 g) of the sugar, the corn syrup, and ¼ cup (60 ml) water and cook, stirring occasionally, until the sugar is dissolved, about 3 minutes. Stop stirring and wash down the sugar crystals on the sides of the pan with a pastry brush dipped in cold water. Continue to cook, swirling the pan occasionally, until the mixture turns a deep golden-brown color and starts to steam. The caramel should be fairly dark, but watch it carefully to prevent it from burning. Immediately pour the caramel into the pie dish and carefully swirl to coat the bottom of the dish evenly. Set the dish aside. The caramel will cool and harden.

Preheat the oven to 325°F (165°C).

In a saucepan over medium heat, warm the milk, half-and-half, orange zest, salt, and remaining ¾ cup (5 oz/140 g) sugar until the milk simmers. Cover, remove from the heat, and set aside for a few minutes. In a bowl, whisk together the eggs and vanilla until combined. Whisking constantly, pour a ladleful of the hot milk mixture into the eggs, then pour the egg mixture into the hot milk mixture in the saucepan.

Pour the custard through a fine-mesh sieve into the pie dish with the caramel. Place the dish in the baking pan and carefully pour hot water into the pan until it reaches about halfway up the sides of the pie dish. Bake until the custard is mostly set but the center still jiggles slightly, about 1 hour.

Carefully remove the pie dish from the water bath, place on a wire rack, and let cool to room temperature. Press plastic wrap directly onto the surface of the custard and refrigerate until chilled, at least 4 hours or up to overnight.

To serve, run a small knife around the inside edge of the dish. Invert a flat serving plate on top of the dish, then invert the dish and plate together. Lift off the dish and cut the flan into wedges.

blueberry cheesecake squares
with hazelnut crust

Toasty hazelnuts add earthiness and depth to the graham cracker crust in these crave-worthy bars, while fresh blueberries folded into the cream cheese filling provide both flavor and texture. Make these bars a day in advance, wrap individual bars in parchment, and pack them along on your next summer adventure.

FOR THE
HAZELNUT CRUST

½ cup (2½ oz/70 g) skinned
hazelnuts, toasted (page 74)

1 cup (3½ oz/100 g)
graham cracker crumbs
(about 8 crackers)

¼ cup (1¾ oz/50 g) sugar

⅛ teaspoon salt

5 tablespoons (2½ oz/75 g)
unsalted butter, melted, plus
more for greasing

FOR THE FILLING

1 lb (450 g) cream cheese,
at room temperature

¾ cup (5 oz/140 g) sugar

2 tablespoons
all-purpose flour

3 large eggs

¼ cup (60 ml) heavy cream

2 teaspoons vanilla extract

1½ cups (7½ oz/210 g)
fresh blueberries

MAKES 9 SQUARES

Preheat the oven to 325°F (165°C). Grease a 9-inch (23-cm) square baking pan. Line the pan with parchment paper, allowing a 2-inch (7-cm) overhang on two of the sides. Lightly butter the parchment.

To make the crust, in a food processor, process the nuts until finely ground. Add the graham cracker crumbs, sugar, and salt and process until the mixture is finely ground. Add the butter and process until evenly moistened. Pour the mixture into the prepared pan and gently press it evenly into the bottom and about 1 inch (2.5 cm) up the sides of the pan. Bake until the crust is golden and looks dry and firm, about 10 minutes. Transfer the pan to a wire rack and let cool completely.

To make the filling, in the clean bowl of the food processor, process the cream cheese and sugar until blended and smooth. Add the flour and process until blended. Add the eggs one at a time, processing after each addition until well combined. Stop the processor and scrape down the sides of the bowl. Add the cream and vanilla and process until well combined. Remove the blade and, using a rubber spatula, stir in the blueberries. Pour the filling into the crust and spread evenly.

Bake until the center barely jiggles when the pan is gently shaken, 30–35 minutes. Let cool on a wire rack for 1 hour. Cover with plastic wrap and refrigerate until chilled, at least 3 hours or up to overnight. Gently remove the cheesecake by lifting the two sides of parchment. Cut into 9 squares and serve.

apricot-almond crisp

Apricots and almonds have a natural affinity for each other, highlighted in this dessert. Crisps, so named for the crunchy oat-based topping, are a terrific way to showcase whatever fruit is in season. If apricots are not your thing, try sliced peaches, nectarines, or apples. Adjust the amount of tapioca starch in the filling based on the juiciness of the fruit, and bake until the filling is tender and bubbling.

FOR THE OAT TOPPING

1 cup (3½ oz/100 g)
quick-cooking rolled oats

1 cup (3 oz/90 g)
sliced almonds

½ cup (2 oz/60 g)
all-purpose flour

½ cup (3½ oz/100 g) firmly
packed light brown sugar

½ teaspoon ground cinnamon

½ teaspoon ground ginger

¼ teaspoon salt

½ cup (4 oz/115 g) cold
unsalted butter, melted,
plus more for greasing

FOR THE
APRICOT FILLING

¾ cup (5 oz/140 g)
granulated sugar

2 teaspoons tapioca starch

Pinch of salt

2½ lb (1 kg) apricots,
pitted and diced

MAKES 8 SERVINGS

Preheat the oven to 350°F (180°C). Grease a 2-qt (2-L) baking dish or 9-by-13-inch (23-by-33-cm) rectangular baking dish.

To make the topping, in a bowl, stir together the oats, almonds, flour, brown sugar, cinnamon, ginger, and salt. Stir in the butter until the mixture is evenly moistened and crumbly. Cover and refrigerate while you prepare the filling.

To make the filling, in a small bowl, stir together the granulated sugar, tapioca starch, and salt. Place the apricots in a large bowl, sprinkle with the sugar mixture, and toss to distribute evenly. Spread the apricot mixture in the prepared baking dish. Sprinkle the topping evenly over the apricots.

Bake until the topping is crisp and golden brown and the apricot filling bubbles slowly, about 50 minutes. Serve warm.

peach streusel pie

There's little better than biting into a ripe peach on a hot summer day when the sweet juices run down your chin. Take advantage of peaches at their peak by making this all-American pie. Top with crunchy streusel, or make a double-crust pie, topping it with a round of dough instead of the streusel. To peel peaches, blanch them quickly in boiling water and the skins should slip right off with little effort.

1 recipe Flaky Pie Dough, Single Crust (page 166)

¾ cup (5 oz/140 g) sugar

3 tablespoons tapioca starch

Pinch of salt

6 or 7 ripe but firm peaches, peeled, pitted, and sliced ½ inch (12 mm) thick

FOR THE STREUSEL

1 cup (4¼ oz/120 g) all-purpose flour

½ cup (3½ oz/100 g) sugar

⅛ teaspoon salt

6 tablespoons (3 oz/90 g) unsalted butter, melted

1 teaspoon vanilla extract

MAKES 8 SERVINGS

Prepare the dough and chill as directed. On a lightly floured work surface, roll out the dough into a round at least 12 inches (30 cm) in diameter and about ⅛ inch (3 mm) thick. Transfer to a 9-inch (23-cm) pie pan and ease into the pan. Trim the overhang to 1 inch (2.5 cm), fold the edge of the dough under itself to create a rim, and crimp the edges to seal. Prick the bottom of the crust all over with a fork and freeze for 30 minutes.

Place a rack in the lower third of the oven and preheat to 375°F (190°C).

In a small bowl, stir together the sugar, tapioca starch, and salt. Place the peaches in a large bowl, sprinkle with the sugar mixture, and toss to distribute evenly.

To make the streusel, in a bowl, combine the flour, sugar, and salt and stir together with a fork. Add the butter and vanilla and stir until evenly blended and crumbly.

Pour the filling into the crust. Top evenly with the streusel. Place the pie dish on a baking sheet and bake until the filling is thick and bubbling and the top is golden, about 1 hour. Transfer to a wire rack and let cool completely to set before serving.

honey pistachio baklava

Crisp honeyed baklava filled with ground nuts—either walnuts or pistachios or a mixture of both—is a specialty of the Middle East and the Mediterranean. Here, spiced ground pistachios fill buttered filo layers, which are baked and then doused with honey syrup. Be sure to let the baklava sit for at least a day before serving to soak up all the honey goodness.

2½ cups (10 oz/390 g) unsalted pistachios, chopped, plus 3 tablespoons

¾ cup (5 oz/150 g) sugar, plus 3 tablespoons

1 teaspoon ground cinnamon

¼ teaspoon salt

1 lb (450 g) filo dough, thawed if frozen

½ cup (4 oz/115 g) unsalted butter, melted

1 cup (8½ oz/340 g) honey

MAKES ABOUT 36 PIECES

In a food processor, combine the 2½ cups (10 oz/390 g) pistachios, the 3 tablespoons sugar, the cinnamon, and salt and pulse until finely ground. Transfer to a bowl.

Lay the filo dough flat on a cutting board with the long side of the rectangle facing you. Cut the stack of sheets in half vertically to make 2 rectangles, each roughly 8 by 12 inches (20 by 30 cm). Pile the sheets in a single stack and cover with a sheet of plastic wrap, then lay a dampened dish towel over the plastic.

Brush a 9-by-13-inch (23-by-33-cm) baking dish with melted butter. Place 1 filo sheet in the dish and brush it with melted butter, working from the edges to the center. Repeat to make 12 layers. Sprinkle about one-fourth of the nut mixture over the top sheet of filo, then top with 2 more buttered filo sheets. Sprinkle another fourth of the nut mixture over the top sheet of filo, followed by 2 more buttered filo sheets. Repeat once more, using half of the remaining nut mixture. Finish with the remaining nut mixture and all of the remaining filo sheets, brushing each with butter. Brush the top sheet with the remaining butter and refrigerate the dish for 15 minutes.

Preheat the oven to 350°F (180°C). Using a thin, serrated knife, cut the baklava into 18 rectangles (3 across the short side and 6 down the long side), and then cut each rectangle diagonally to form 2 triangles. Bake until golden brown, 50–60 minutes. Transfer to a wire rack and let cool.

In a small saucepan over medium heat, bring the ¾ cup (5 oz/150 g) sugar and ½ cup (120 ml) water to a boil, stirring to dissolve the sugar. Boil, without stirring, until the mixture registers 220°F (104°C) on a candy thermometer, about 5 minutes. Remove from the heat and stir in the honey to make a syrup.

Carefully pour the syrup evenly over the warm baklava. Sprinkle with the 3 tablespoons pistachios. Cover loosely with parchment paper and let stand at room temperature for at least 8 hours or up to overnight.

To serve, run a knife along the cuts and then remove the pieces.

lemon meringue pie with gingersnap crust

This updated version of lemon meringue pie uses a spicy gingersnap crumb crust instead of the classic pastry dough. If you want a more traditional pie, prebake a pie shell (see page 169) before adding the filling. For another modern twist, swap out the regular lemon juice for Meyer lemon juice, which will add a sweeter floral note to the pie.

1 recipe Gingersnap Crust (page 169)

FOR THE
LEMON CURD FILLING

5 large eggs, plus 7 large egg yolks (save 5 egg whites for the meringue)

1½ cups (10½ oz/300 g) sugar

⅓ cup (1½ oz/40 g) cornstarch

1½ cups (360 ml) fresh lemon juice

¼ teaspoon salt

½ cup (4 oz/115 g) unsalted butter, cut into cubes

FOR THE MERINGUE

5 large egg whites

¼ teaspoon cream of tartar

½ cup (3½ oz/100 g) sugar

½ teaspoon vanilla extract

MAKES 8 SERVINGS

Make the gingersnap crust and bake as directed.

To make the filling, in a saucepan over medium-high heat, whisk together the eggs, egg yolks, sugar, cornstarch, lemon juice, and salt. Cook, stirring constantly, until the mixture comes to a boil. Reduce the heat to medium and cook, stirring constantly, until thickened, 6–8 minutes.

Pour the mixture through a fine-mesh sieve into a large bowl. Add the butter and stir until melted. Let cool to room temperature. Spread the filling over the crust. Press plastic wrap directly onto the surface of the curd and refrigerate for at least 1 hour or up to overnight.

To make the meringue, in a large bowl, using an electric mixer on medium speed, beat together the egg whites and cream of tartar until foamy, about 2 minutes. Raise the speed to medium-high and slowly add the sugar. Beat until soft peaks form and the egg whites are shiny and glossy, about 3 minutes. Add the vanilla and beat until the egg whites hold stiff peaks, about 1 minute longer.

Preheat the broiler or have ready a kitchen torch. Place the pie dish on a baking sheet. Pipe or spread the meringue over the lemon curd filling so that it completely covers the pie, leaving no gaps between the crust and the meringue. Broil until the meringue is lightly toasted, about 5 minutes; alternatively, use the kitchen torch to brown the meringue. Refrigerate for at least 2 hours or up to overnight before serving.

cherry lattice pie

Fresh sour cherries have a fleeting season in late spring and early summer, so most recipes opt for jarred or canned varieties. Choose a good-quality brand with no added sugars so you can control the sweetness. If you substitute sweet cherries, be sure to decrease the amount of sugar slightly.

1 recipe Flaky Pie Dough, Double Crust (page 166)

1 cup (7 oz/200 g) sugar

2 tablespoons tapioca starch

⅛ teaspoon salt

4 cups (10 oz/315 g) drained jarred or canned pitted sour cherries, plus ⅓ cup (80 ml) cherry liquid

1 teaspoon vanilla extract

1 tablespoon cold unsalted butter, cut into small pieces

MAKES 8 SERVINGS

Prepare the dough and chill as directed. On a lightly floured work surface, roll out each dough half into a round at least 12 inches (30 cm) in diameter and about ⅛ inch (3 mm) thick. Transfer one round to a 9-inch (23-cm) pie pan and ease into the pan. Trim the overhang to 1 inch (2.5 cm). Refrigerate the pie shell and the remaining dough while you prepare the filling.

In a small bowl, stir together the sugar, tapioca starch, and salt. Place the cherries in a large bowl, sprinkle with the sugar mixture, and toss to distribute evenly. Add the cherry liquid and the vanilla and mix well. Pour the filling into the crust and dot with the butter.

Lay the second dough round on a lightly floured work surface and, using a 1-inch-wide (2.5-cm-wide) ruler as a guide, cut 9–10 strips of dough. Lay 5 strips of dough evenly across the top of the pie, using the longest strips in the center. Lay the remaining 4 or 5 strips perpendicular to the other strips, spacing them evenly. (You can also weave together the strips.) Trim the ends of the strips and tuck the dough under itself to create a rim. Crimp the edges with your fingers or a fork. Refrigerate until the dough is firm, at least 30 minutes.

Preheat the oven to 375°F (190°C). Bake until the crust is golden and the filling is thick and bubbling, 45–60 minutes. Transfer the pie to a wire rack and let cool completely to set the filling, then serve.

cinnamon-sugar churros

Crispy deep-fried churros hail from Spain, where they are served alongside thick, rich hot chocolate for dipping. Made from a choux-like dough that is piped into hot oil, the just-fried doughnuts are then tossed in cinnamon-sugar for a delicious coating. Eat them while they are still warm!

¼ teaspoon salt

3 tablespoons sugar

1 cup (4¼ oz/120 g) all-purpose flour, sifted

2 large eggs, beaten

Peanut or canola oil for deep-frying

1 long strip lemon peel

1 tablespoon ground cinnamon

MAKES 6 SERVINGS

In a saucepan over high heat, bring 1 cup (240 ml) water, the salt, and 1 tablespoon of the sugar to a boil. Remove from the heat and immediately add the flour. Stir with a wooden spoon until the dough is very smooth and pulls away from the sides of the pan, about 2 minutes. Let cool for 5 minutes, then, using an electric mixer, beat in the eggs about 1 tablespoon at a time. Spoon the dough into a pastry bag fitted with a large star tip.

Line a baking sheet with paper towels. Pour the oil to a depth of 1 inch (2.5 cm) into a deep, heavy frying pan and warm over medium heat until it registers 350°F (180°C) on a deep-frying thermometer. Add the lemon peel and cook until browned, about 5 minutes; discard. Pipe several strips of dough, each 3–4 inches (7.5–10 cm) long, directly into the hot oil, being careful not to crowd the pan. Using a small knife, cut the strips free of the piping tip, dipping the knife in the oil before each cut. Fry the churros, using tongs to turn them as needed, until golden brown and crisp, 3–5 minutes. Transfer the churros to the paper towels to drain briefly, then place them in a large bowl. Continue to fry the remaining dough in batches.

In a small bowl, stir together the cinnamon and the remaining 2 tablespoons sugar. Sprinkle over the churros and toss to coat, then serve.

honey-nectarine cheesecake

This delicate honey-sweetened cheesecake is a natural partner to fragrant nectarines. Once you bake the crust to set it, the rest of the preparation is oven-free, making this a great dessert for a hot day. Brushing the nectarine slices with melted jam gives them a professional gloss, but skip this step for a more rustic look.

FOR THE CRUST

1 cup (3 oz/90 g) sliced almonds, lightly toasted (see Note)

1 cup (3½ oz/100 g) graham cracker crumbs (about 8 crackers)

¼ cup (2 oz/60 g) firmly packed light brown sugar

5 tablespoons (2½ oz/75 g) unsalted butter, melted

FOR THE FILLING AND TOPPING

2 lb (1 kg) cream cheese

⅓ cup (3 oz/115 g) honey

¼ cup (1¾ oz/50 g) granulated sugar

1 cup (250 ml) heavy cream

2 tablespoons fresh lemon juice

½ teaspoon almond extract

1 teaspoon unflavored gelatin

3 tablespoons apricot or peach jam

4 ripe nectarines, about 1½ lb (750 g), pitted and sliced

MAKES 8–10 SERVINGS

Preheat the oven to 350°F (180°C).

To make the crust, in a food processor, combine the almonds, graham cracker crumbs, and brown sugar and process until finely ground. Add the butter and process until the crumbs begin to stick together. Gently press the crust mixture evenly into the bottom and 2 inches (5 cm) up the sides of a 9-inch (23-cm) springform pan. Bake until the crust is set, about 10 minutes. Let cool completely.

To make the filling, in a large bowl, using an electric mixer on medium speed, beat the cream cheese, honey, and granulated sugar until smooth. Beat in ½ cup (125 ml) of the cream, the lemon juice, and the almond extract. Place 1 tablespoon water in a small saucepan. Sprinkle the gelatin over the surface and let soften for 5 minutes. Place the pan over low heat and stir until the gelatin dissolves. Gradually whisk in the remaining ½ cup (125 ml) cream. Add the gelatin mixture to the cream cheese mixture and beat until fluffy, about 1 minute. Spoon the filling into the crust. Cover and refrigerate overnight or up to 2 days.

To serve, remove the pan sides and, using a spatula, transfer the cake to a plate. In a small saucepan over medium heat, stir the jam until melted. Let cool slightly. Arrange the nectarine slices on the cheesecake. Using a pastry brush, brush the melted jam over the fruit. Cut the cake into wedges and serve.

NOTE *To toast nuts, such as almonds, hazelnuts, walnuts, or pecans, or shredded or flaked dried coconut, preheat the oven to 325°F (165°C). Spread the nuts or coconut in a single layer on a rimmed baking sheet and toast, stirring occasionally, until fragrant and lightly golden, 5–10 minutes for coconut and 10–20 minutes for nuts. To skin hazelnuts, rub the warm toasted nuts in a kitchen towel.*

blueberry-lemon drizzle cake

With a triple dose of lemon—zest in the cake, a syrup brushed on while the cake is warm, and a glaze drizzled over the top—this loaf cake is definitely designed for lemon lovers. The blueberries add texture and sweetness. For a lemon–poppy seed cake, omit the blueberries and add 1 tablespoon poppy seeds to the flour mixture.

FOR THE
BLUEBERRY CAKE

1½ cups (6½ oz/180 g)
all-purpose flour, plus
1 teaspoon

1 teaspoon baking powder

¼ teaspoon salt

½ cup (4 oz/115 g)
unsalted butter, at cool
room temperature

¾ cup (5 oz/140 g)
granulated sugar

1 tablespoon finely grated
lemon zest

3 large eggs

½ cup (125 ml) whole milk

1 teaspoon vanilla extract

1 cup (5 oz/140 g)
fresh blueberries

FOR THE LEMON SYRUP

3 tablespoons fresh
lemon juice

3 tablespoons
granulated sugar

FOR THE LEMON GLAZE

½ cup (2 oz/60 g)
confectioners' sugar

3 teaspoons fresh lemon juice

MAKES 8 SERVINGS

Preheat the oven to 350°F (180°C). Grease a 9-by-5-inch (23-by-13-cm) loaf pan with nonstick cooking spray.

To make the cake, in a bowl, sift together the 1½ cups (6½ oz/180 g) flour, the baking powder, and salt. In a bowl, using an electric mixer on medium-high speed, beat the butter, granulated sugar, and lemon zest until light and fluffy, 2–3 minutes. Add the eggs one at a time and beat until incorporated. Add the milk and vanilla and stir until blended. Add the baking powder mixture and stir just until blended. In a small bowl, toss the blueberries and the 1 teaspoon flour until coated. Using a rubber spatula, gently fold the berries into the batter.

Scrape the batter into the prepared pan and spread evenly. Bake until lightly browned and a toothpick inserted into the center comes out clean, about 50 minutes. Transfer the pan to a wire rack set over a rimmed baking sheet and let the cake cool in the pan for a few minutes, then turn out onto the rack.

While the bread is baking, make the syrup: In a small saucepan over medium heat, boil the lemon juice and granulated sugar until syrupy, about 2 minutes. Remove from the heat.

While the bread is still warm, using a toothpick, pierce the sides and bottom of the bread all over. Brush the bread generously with the syrup.

To make the glaze, in a small bowl, stir together the confectioners' sugar and lemon juice. When the bread is completely cool, drizzle the glaze over the top. Serve thick slices.

strawberry shortcakes

A hint of lemon zest in these tender shortcakes adds delicate flavor and is a perfect partner to succulent sugared strawberries and vanilla whipped cream. Be careful not to overwork the dough so it stays nice and tender—let it stay a little rough, even shaggy. Cutting the dough into squares means fewer scraps, but if you like neat round shortcakes, use a 3-inch (7.5-cm) round cutter to cut out six cakes (you will need to pat the scraps together).

FOR THE SHORTCAKES

2 cups (9 oz/240 g)
all-purpose flour,
plus more for dusting

2 tablespoons sugar, plus
more for sprinkling

1 tablespoon baking powder

½ teaspoon salt

1 teaspoon finely grated
lemon zest

6 tablespoons (3 oz/90 g)
cold unsalted butter,
cut into small pieces

1 cup (250 ml) heavy cream,
plus more for brushing

FOR THE FILLING

2 pints (1 lb/450 g) fresh
strawberries, hulled and
sliced or halved

¼ cup (1¾ oz/50 g) sugar

1 recipe Whipped Cream
(page 176)

MAKES 6 SERVINGS

Preheat the oven to 400°F (200°C). Line a baking sheet with parchment paper.

To make the shortcakes, in a bowl, whisk together the flour, sugar, baking powder, salt, and lemon zest until well blended. Using a pastry blender or 2 knives, cut in the butter until the pieces are about the size of peas. Add the cream and gently toss with a fork until the flour is just moistened and the ingredients are blended. Turn the dough out onto a lightly floured work surface. Gently pat the dough into a thick rectangle about 6 by 4 inches (15 by 10 cm). Trim the edges to make them even, then cut the rectangle into 6 equal squares.

Place the shortcakes on the prepared baking sheet, spacing them well apart. Brush each with a little cream, then sprinkle with sugar. Bake until puffed and golden, 15–18 minutes. Transfer the shortcakes to a wire rack to cool slightly.

Meanwhile, make the filling: in a bowl, toss together the strawberries and sugar with a fork, lightly crushing some of the berries. Let stand until ready to serve.

Split the shortcakes in half horizontally and place the bottom halves, cut side up, on plates. Spoon some of the filling over each half and top with a dollop of whipped cream. Top with the remaining shortcake halves, cut side down, and serve.

piñata cupcakes

Perfect for a party, tender vanilla cupcakes are filled with a pile of fun sprinkles that are only revealed with the first bite. A pretty swirl of blue and pink buttercream tops each treat, but you can use your favorite colors or match them to your party theme.

FOR THE VANILLA
CUPCAKES

1¼ cups (5½ oz/155 g)
all-purpose flour

1¼ teaspoons baking powder

¼ teaspoon salt

¾ cup (5 oz/140 g) sugar

6 tablespoons (3 oz/90 g)
unsalted butter, at cool
room temperature

2 large eggs

1 teaspoon vanilla extract

⅓ cup (80 ml) whole milk

½ cup star-shaped
or other sprinkles

Blue and pink gel
food coloring

1 recipe Fluffy Vanilla
Frosting (page 171)

MAKES 12 CUPCAKES

Preheat the oven to 350°F (180°C). Line 12 standard muffin cups with paper or foil liners.

To make the cupcakes, in a medium bowl, whisk together the flour, baking powder, and salt.

In a large bowl, using an electric mixer on medium-high speed, beat the sugar and butter until light and fluffy, 2–3 minutes. Add the eggs one at a time, beating well after each addition. Turn off the mixer and scrape down the sides of the bowl. Add the vanilla and beat until combined. Reduce the speed to low, add about half of the flour mixture, and mix just until blended. Add the milk and mix until combined. Add the remaining flour mixture and mix just until blended. Turn off the mixer, scrape down the sides of the bowl, and give the batter a final stir with the spatula.

Divide the batter evenly among the prepared muffin cups. Bake until the tops are light golden brown and a toothpick inserted into the center of a cupcake comes out clean, 18–20 minutes. Transfer the pan to a wire rack and let cool for 10 minutes. Remove the cupcakes from the pans and let cool completely on the rack, about 1 hour.

Using a paring knife, cut a 1½-inch (4-cm) round about 1 inch (2.5 cm) deep in the center of each cupcake, then remove the rounds and set them aside. Fill each hollow with about 2 teaspoons of sprinkles. Cut the rounds that you removed from the cupcakes in half horizontally; reserve the tops and discard—or eat!—the rest. Return the tops to the cupcakes, covering the sprinkles, then gently press down on each to fit it into the hole.

Fit a large pastry bag with a large star tip. Using a paintbrush, paint a stripe of blue food coloring from tip to top against the inside of the pastry bag, then paint another blue stripe against the other side of the bag, opposite the first stripe. Clean the brush and paint a stripe of pink food coloring against the side of the pastry bag between the blue stripes, then paint a second pink stripe opposite the first pink stripe. Transfer the frosting to the pastry bag; try not to disturb the stripes. Pipe the frosting onto the cupcakes and serve.

chocolate mint chip ice cream cake

You can personalize this celebratory treat to suit any flavor of ice cream that would pair well with chocolate cake—mint chip, strawberry, or caramel would all be terrific. Instead of sprinkles, top with crushed chocolate wafer cookies or chocolate-almond toffee.

FOR THE
CHOCOLATE CAKE

1 cup (4¼ oz/120 g)
all-purpose flour

¼ cup (¾ oz/20 g)
unsweetened Dutch-process
cocoa powder

2 teaspoons baking powder

¼ teaspoon salt

¾ cup (5 oz/140 g) sugar

1 large egg

⅓ cup (80 ml) avocado or
canola oil

1 tablespoon vanilla extract

FOR THE FILLING

1 cup (4¼ oz/120 g) 2 qt (2 L)
mint chip ice cream, slightly
softened

1 recipe Whipped Cream
(page 176)

Chocolate or rainbow sprinkles,
for decorating (optional)

MAKES 10–12 SERVINGS

Preheat the oven to 325°F (165°C). Grease a 9-by-13-inch (23-by-33-cm) baking dish.

To make the cake, in a large bowl, sift together the flour, cocoa, baking powder, and salt. Whisk in the sugar. In another bowl, whisk together ¾ cup (180 ml) warm water, the egg, oil, and vanilla until blended. Pour the egg mixture into the dry ingredients and stir with the whisk just until blended. Pour the batter into the prepared dish. Bake until a toothpick inserted into the center of the cake comes out clean, about 20 minutes. Transfer the pan to a wire rack and let cool completely.

Drop large spoonfuls of the ice cream over the top of the cake and spread to make a thick, even layer. Cover with plastic wrap and freeze until the ice cream is hard, about 4 hours.

Spread the whipped cream over the frozen cake and top with sprinkles, if using. Cut into squares and serve.

summer peach-raspberry muffins

The combination of sweet summer peaches and tart raspberries makes these muffins a terrific morning treat. They are based on the classic dessert peach melba, where poached peach halves are topped with ice cream and raspberry sauce. These muffins are gilded with sugared toasted almonds which you can leave off if you like.

2 cups (9 oz/240 g) all-purpose flour

½ cup (3½ oz/100 g) sugar, plus 1 tablespoon

2 teaspoons baking powder

½ teaspoon salt

1 cup (250 ml) whole milk

2 large eggs

6 tablespoons (3 oz/90 g) unsalted butter, melted

1 large ripe peach (8 oz/225 g), peeled, pitted, and finely chopped

1 cup (4 oz/115 g) fresh raspberries, halved

¼ cup (¾ oz/25 g) sliced almonds

MAKES 16 MUFFINS

Preheat the oven to 400°F (200°C). Line 16 cups of two standard muffin pans with paper liners or grease with nonstick cooking spray.

In a small bowl, whisk together the flour, the ½ cup (3½ oz/100 g) sugar, baking powder, and salt. In a large bowl, whisk together the milk, eggs, and butter until blended. Using a rubber spatula, stir in the flour mixture just until evenly moistened. Gently fold in the peach and raspberries just until evenly distributed. Do not overmix.

Divide the batter among the prepared muffin cups, filling each three-fourths full. Sprinkle each with the sliced almonds and the 1 tablespoon sugar, dividing evenly.

Bake until golden and a toothpick inserted into the center comes out dry, 25–30 minutes. Transfer the pan to a wire rack and let cool for 5 minutes. Remove the muffins from the pan and let cool on the rack. Serve warm or at room temperature.

vanilla ombré layer cake

This tall four-layer vanilla cake is so gorgeous it's worthy of a grand celebration. Ombré is the gradual blending of one shade into another. Here, the colors fade from dark berry to pink to white. You'll need four cake pans to create this effect, as each layer is a different hue. Once it is layered, the cake is covered in easy-to-pipe rosettes.

2¾ cups (12 oz/330 g) all-purpose flour, plus more for dusting

2½ teaspoons baking powder

¾ teaspoon baking soda

½ teaspoon salt

3 large egg whites, plus 1 large egg

2 cups (14 oz/400 g) sugar

¾ cup (6 oz/170 g) unsalted butter, at cool room temperature, plus more for greasing

1 tablespoon vanilla extract

1½ cups (350 ml) buttermilk

Pink, red, or other food coloring of choice

2 recipes Quick Vanilla Buttercream (page 174)

MAKES 12 SERVINGS

Place 1 rack in the upper third and 1 rack in the lower third of the oven and preheat to 350°F (180°C). Grease four 8-inch (20-cm) round cake pans, line the bottoms of the pans with parchment paper, then butter the parchment. Dust with flour, then tap out any excess.

In a bowl, sift together the flour, baking powder, baking soda, and salt. In a bowl, using an electric mixer on medium-high speed, beat the egg whites until frothy, about 1 minute. Slowly add 1 cup (7 oz/200 g) of the sugar and beat until medium-soft peaks form, about 3 minutes. Set aside.

In another bowl, beat the butter and remaining 1 cup (7 oz/200 g) sugar on medium speed until light and fluffy, about 2 minutes. Add the egg and vanilla and beat until combined, about 1 minute. Stop the mixer and scrape down the sides of the bowl. Reduce the speed to low and add the flour mixture in 3 additions, alternating with the buttermilk and beginning and ending with the flour, and beat until combined. Stop the mixer and scrape down the sides of the bowl, then beat again for 10 seconds. Using a rubber spatula, gently fold the egg white mixture into the batter.

Divide the batter evenly among 4 bowls. Add food coloring to 3 of the bowls, making light, medium, and dark shades of the same color. Stir the batter until the food coloring is completely blended. Leave 1 bowl of batter plain.

Pour each batter into a prepared pan and spread evenly. Bake, rotating the pans between the racks halfway through baking, until a toothpick inserted into the center of the cakes comes out clean, 15–20 minutes. Transfer the pans to wire racks and let cool for 10 minutes, then invert the cakes onto the racks and let cool completely.

Reserve half of the buttercream for the filling, crumb coat, and bottom layer of frosting. Spoon half of the remaining buttercream into a bowl, then add food coloring to make it the darkest shade. Divide the remaining buttercream between 2 bowls and add food coloring to make light and medium shades. Stir the buttercream until the food coloring is completely blended.

To assemble the cake, place the plain cake layer on a cake stand or serving plate. Spread about ¼ cup (115 g) of the plain buttercream evenly over the cake, then top with the lightest dyed cake layer. Repeat with the remaining cake layers, ending with the darkest one. Spread a very thin layer of plain buttercream over the top and sides of the cake. Refrigerate until you are ready to pipe the rosettes.

Transfer the remaining plain buttercream to a large pastry bag fitted with a large star tip. Starting at the bottom of the cake, pipe a single row of rosettes. Repeat with the lightest-colored buttercream (using a clean pastry bag and tip), followed by the medium buttercream. Finally, pipe the darkest shade in a single row of rosettes on the side of the cake and all over the top of the cake. Serve.

summer fruit trifle

Trifle is a British dessert made of layers of cake—which are often doused in some kind of spirit—plus custard, fresh fruit, and whipped cream. It's best if the dessert is assembled at least a few hours in advance to give the layers time to soak into each other. This version, which is perfect for a gathering, is as versatile as summertime fruits, so choose whatever is ripe, fresh, and fragrant.

FOR THE VANILLA
CHIFFON CAKE

1 cup (4¼ oz/120 g) cake flour

1 teaspoon baking powder

½ cup (3½ oz/100 g) sugar

3 tablespoons avocado or canola oil

1 teaspoon vanilla extract

2 large eggs, separated

⅛ teaspoon salt

⅛ teaspoon cream of tartar

5 cups (1½ lb/750 g) diced mixed summer fruit, such as raspberries, blackberries, strawberries, peaches, nectarines, apricots, or cherries

¼–½ cup (3½ oz/100 g) sugar, depending on the sweetness of the fruit

½ cup (120 ml) sweet sherry

1 recipe Vanilla Bean Pastry Cream (page 176)

1 recipe Whipped Cream (page 176)

MAKES 10 SERVINGS

To make the cake, preheat the oven to 350°F (180°C). Line two 9-inch (23-cm) round cake pans with parchment paper.

In a bowl, sift together the flour and baking powder. Whisk in ¼ cup (1¾ oz/50 g) of the sugar. In a large bowl, whisk together the oil, vanilla, egg yolks, and ¼ cup (60 ml) water. In a third bowl, using an electric mixer on medium speed, beat the egg whites, salt, and cream of tartar. When the egg whites get frothy, slowly add the remaining ¼ cup (1¾ oz/50 g) sugar, beating just until stiff peaks form, about 3–5 minutes. Whisk the flour mixture into the oil mixture, then fold the egg whites into the batter. Divide the batter evenly between the prepared pans.

Bake until a toothpick inserted into the center of the cakes comes out clean, 15–18 minutes. Transfer the pans to wire racks and let cool for 15 minutes. Run a thin knife around the edge of the cake pans to loosen the cakes, then invert the cakes onto the rack, peel off the parchment, and let cool completely.

To assemble the trifle, in a bowl, toss the fruit with the sugar to taste and set aside for 20 minutes to macerate. Have ready a trifle bowl or a 3-qt (3-L) glass bowl measuring about 8 inches (20 cm) high and 8 inches (20 cm) in diameter. Cut the cakes crosswise into thick slices (or into chunks).

Line the bottom of the bowl with some of the cake slices. Sprinkle the cake slices generously with half of the sherry, then top with half of the fruit and half of the pastry cream. Top with the remaining cake slices, sherry, fruit, and pastry cream. Cover with plastic wrap and refrigerate for at least 2 hours.

Top the trifle with whipped cream up to 1 hour before serving. Use a large spoon to serve the trifle to make sure you get every layer.

tres leches cake

Tres leches, meaning "three milks," is a tender, luscious cake made throughout Latin America. Here, vanilla cake is soaked in a rich sauce made from condensed milk, evaporated milk, cream, and rum, then spread with fluffy marshmallow-like meringue frosting. Serve thick pieces of cake with sliced pineapple or mango.

FOR THE CAKE

½ cup (4 oz/115 g)
vegetable shortening,
plus more for greasing

1½ cups (10½ oz/300 g) sugar

2 large eggs

2¼ cups (10 oz/270 g) sifted
all-purpose flour

2 teaspoons baking powder

½ teaspoon salt

1 cup (250 ml) whole milk

1 teaspoon vanilla extract

FOR THE
TRES LECHES SAUCE

1 can (14-fl oz) sweetened
condensed milk

1 can (12-fl oz)
evaporated milk

½ cup (125 ml) heavy cream

3 tablespoons dark rum

1 teaspoon vanilla extract

FOR THE
MERINGUE FROSTING

¾ cup (5 oz/140 g) sugar

3 large egg whites

¼ teaspoon cream of tartar

MAKES 10–12 SERVINGS

Preheat the oven to 350°F (180°C). Grease a 9-by-13-inch (23-by-33-cm) baking pan. Dust with flour, then tap out any excess.

To make the cake, in a bowl, using an electric mixer on high speed, beat the shortening until fluffy, about 2 minutes. Add the sugar a little at a time, beating until fluffy after each addition. Reduce the speed to low and add the eggs one at a time, beating until incorporated after each addition. In a large bowl, sift together the flour, baking powder, and salt. In a small bowl, whisk together the milk and vanilla. Add one-third of the milk mixture to the egg mixture and beat until well mixed, then add one-third of the flour mixture. Repeat twice more, beating well after each addition. Scrape the batter into the prepared pan and spread evenly.

Bake until a toothpick inserted into the center of the cake comes out clean, about 35 minutes. Transfer the pan to a wire rack and let cool for 10 minutes, then invert the cake onto a platter and let cool completely.

To make the sauce, in a bowl, whisk together the condensed milk, evaporated milk, cream, rum, and vanilla. Poke the cake all over with a fork, and spoon the sauce over the surface, a little at a time, allowing the cake to absorb the sauce before adding more. A little sauce may pool on the platter. Cover the cake with plastic wrap and refrigerate for about 1 hour.

To make the frosting, in a saucepan over medium-high heat, bring the sugar and ½ cup (120 ml) water to a boil, stirring to dissolve the sugar. Reduce the heat and simmer until it registers 230°F (110°C) on a candy thermometer, 10–12 minutes. Wash down the sugar crystals on the sides of the pan with a pastry brush dipped in cold water. While the sugar is cooking, in a clean metal bowl, using an electric mixer on high speed, beat the egg whites and cream of tartar until stiff peaks form. Slowly add the boiling syrup in a thin stream to the beaten egg whites until all the syrup is incorporated. Continue beating until the frosting is cooled and glossy. Spread the frosting over the cake, cover, and refrigerate until well chilled, at least 3 hours and up to 8 hours. Serve chilled, cut into squares.

red, white & blue bundt cake

A single sour cream batter is transformed into a colorful swirled Bundt cake with just a little red and blue food coloring—making it ideal for a Fourth of July celebration. You can use any Bundt pan design, but be sure to grease and flour it generously so the cake comes out of the pan cleanly.

FOR THE BUNDT CAKE

3 cups (12¾ oz/360 g) cake flour

¼ teaspoon baking soda

¼ teaspoon salt

1 cup (8 oz/225 g) unsalted butter, at cool room temperature, plus more for greasing

2½ cups (17½ oz/500 g) sugar

6 large eggs, at room temperature

2 teaspoons vanilla extract

1 cup (8 oz/225 g) sour cream

Red and blue gel food coloring

FOR DECORATING

 1 recipe Vanilla Icing (page 170)

Red, white, and/or blue sprinkles, for decorating

MAKES 12–16 SERVINGS

Preheat the oven to 325°F (165°C). Grease a 10-inch (25-cm) Bundt pan. Dust with flour, then tap out any excess.

In a bowl, stir together the flour, baking soda, and salt. In another bowl, using an electric mixer on medium-high speed, beat the butter and sugar until fluffy, about 5 minutes. Beat in the eggs one at a time until combined, then beat in the vanilla. Stop the mixer and scrape down the sides of the bowl. Reduce the speed to low and add the flour mixture in 3 additions, alternating with the sour cream and beginning and ending with the flour, beating just until blended after each addition.

Scoop a heaping 1 cup of the batter into a bowl. Then scoop a heaping 1 cup of the batter into another bowl. Transfer the remaining batter to the prepared Bundt pan, spreading it evenly. Add red food coloring to the batter in one bowl, and blue food coloring to the batter in the other bowl, stirring each until well mixed and the shade you desire.

Spoon the red batter in blobs over the plain batter in the Bundt pan, then spoon the blue batter in blobs between the red batter blobs. To marble the batter, draw a toothpick or chopstick through the batter in a series of figure eights.

Bake until a toothpick inserted near the center of the cake comes out clean, 1¼–1½ hours. Transfer the pan to a wire rack and let cool for 10 minutes, then invert the pan onto the rack, lift off the pan, and let cool completely.

Drizzle the icing over the cake so it runs down the sides. Scatter sprinkles on top to decorate. Let the icing set for at least 30 minutes. Cut into slices and serve.

triple-decker birthday cake

This decadent towering cake is a true classic: three layers of yellow butter cake paired with raspberry jam and gooey fudge frosting. It's spectacular enough for any lucky recipient's birthday. When frosting a layer cake, place each layer top side down, as the bottom is generally flatter and easier to frost. If your cake layer is a little lopsided, use a bread knife to trim it until even.

FOR THE
YELLOW BUTTER CAKE

2¾ cups (12 oz/330 g)
cake flour

3 teaspoons baking powder

½ teaspoon salt

1 cup (8 oz/225 g) unsalted butter, at cool room temperature, plus more for greasing

1¾ cups (12 oz/340 g) sugar

4 large eggs, plus 2 large egg yolks

2 teaspoons vanilla extract

1 cup (8 oz/225 g) sour cream

1 recipe Fudge Frosting (page 171)

⅔ cup (6 oz/190 g) raspberry jam

MAKES 12–16 SERVINGS

Preheat the oven to 350°F (180°C). Grease three 9-inch (23-cm) round cake pans, line the bottoms of the pans with parchment paper, then grease the parchment. Dust with flour, then tap out any excess.

To make the cake, in a small bowl, sift together the flour, baking powder, and salt.

In another bowl, using an electric mixer on medium-high speed, beat the butter and sugar until fluffy, about 3 minutes. Add the eggs and egg yolks one at a time, beating well after each addition. Beat in the vanilla. Reduce the speed to low and add half of the flour mixture, then the sour cream, and then the remaining flour mixture, beating until combined.

Divide the batter evenly among the prepared pans and spread evenly. Bake until a toothpick inserted into the center of the cakes comes out clean, 15–20 minutes. Transfer the pans to wire racks and let cool for 15 minutes, then invert the cakes onto the racks, peel off the parchment, and let cool before frosting.

To frost the cake, place one layer, top side down, on a flat serving plate. With an icing spatula, spread the top with a thin layer of frosting. Spread half of the raspberry jam over the frosting. Top with a second cake layer and top that with a thin layer of frosting and the remaining jam. Top with the third cake layer. Cover the top and sides of the cake with a thick layer of the remaining frosting. Serve right away, cut into fat wedges, or keep covered at room temperature until ready to serve.

berries & cream roulade

A mixture of whipped crème fraîche and cream and an array of fresh summer berries are the filling for this delicate roulade cake. Don't let the idea of a roulade, or rolled cake, scare you. By "training" the cake and rolling it just after baking, the likelihood of cracks decreases. But if the cake does crack, the whipped cream filling is great for hiding any blemishes.

FOR THE CAKE

4 large eggs

⅓ cup (2½ oz/70 g) granulated sugar, plus 1 tablespoon

¼ cup (1 oz/30 g) cake flour

FOR THE FILLING

1¾ cups (430 ml) heavy cream

¾ cup (6 oz/180 g) crème fraîche

1 cup (4 oz/115 g) mixed berries, such as whole raspberries, blackberries, or blueberries, or sliced strawberries, plus 15 whole or sliced berries for garnish

1 tablespoon confectioners' sugar

MAKES 8–10 SERVINGS

Preheat the oven to 475°F (245°C). Grease a jelly roll pan, then line the pan with parchment paper.

To make the cake, separate 2 of the eggs. Put the egg whites in a medium bowl and set aside.

Put the egg yolks and remaining 2 eggs into a large mixing bowl. Using an electric mixer on medium speed, beat the eggs while slowly adding the ⅓ cup (2½ oz/70 g) granulated sugar in a steady stream. Raise the speed to high and beat until the eggs are almost doubled in volume, about 5 minutes.

Using clean beaters, beat the egg whites on medium speed until they start to foam. While beating, slowly add the 1 tablespoon granulated sugar. Raise the speed to high and beat until the whites form soft peaks but still look wet. Carefully fold the whites into the egg yolk mixture. Sift the flour over the egg mixture and gently fold in with a rubber spatula. Spread the batter evenly in the prepared pan.

Bake until the cake is springy to the touch, 5–8 minutes, rotating the pan halfway through. Run a table knife around the edge and slide the cake, still on the paper, onto a wire rack. Gently roll up the cake into a log (this will "train" it to not crack when you finish the roulade). Let cool completely.

To make the filling, whip ¾ cup (180 ml) of the cream and the crème fraîche to soft peaks. Gently fold in the 1 cup (4 oz/115 g) berries. Gently unroll the cake onto another piece of parchment paper, peeling off the original paper. Spread the whipped cream mixture onto the cake and roll the cake into a log. Transfer, seam side down, to a serving plate.

Whip the remaining 1 cup (250 ml) cream and the confectioners' sugar to soft peaks. Spoon into a pastry bag fitted with a ¾-inch (2-cm) star tip, and pipe a spiral down the center of the cake. Garnish with the remaining whole berries. Refrigerate until ready to serve.

fall

pumpkin whoopie pies

Whoopie pies—the cake-like cookie sandwiches that bear no resemblance to a pie—elicit cries of delight, no matter what flavor they might be. The classic version is chocolate with a marshmallowy filling, but this one is as autumnal as it gets: tender spiced pumpkin cookies filled with a rich cream cheese frosting. Bring on the pumpkin spice!

1½ cups (6½ oz/180 g) all-purpose flour

1 tablespoon pumpkin spice

1 teaspoon ground cinnamon

½ teaspoon baking powder

½ teaspoon baking soda

½ teaspoon salt

1 can (15-oz) pumpkin purée (about 1½ cups)

½ cup (125 ml) avocado or canola oil

1 large egg

1 teaspoon vanilla extract

1⅓ cups (10¼ oz/290 g) firmly packed dark brown sugar

1 recipe Cream Cheese Frosting (page 173)

MAKES 12 WHOOPIE PIES

Preheat the oven to 350°F (180°C). Line 2 baking sheets with parchment paper.

In a medium bowl, whisk together the flour, pumpkin pie spice, cinnamon, baking powder, baking soda, and salt. Set aside.

In a large bowl, whisk together the pumpkin purée, oil, egg, vanilla, and brown sugar. Sprinkle the flour mixture over the pumpkin mixture and whisk just until combined. Place a pastry bag fitted with a ½-inch (12-mm) round tip in a tall drinking glass. Pour the batter into the bag and twist the top to close it. (Alternatively, use a zippered plastic bag or disposable pastry bag and cut off the tip of the bag to make a ½-inch (12-mm) opening.) Pipe 24 rounds, each 2 inches (5 cm) wide, onto the prepared baking sheets, spacing the rounds at least 1 inch (2.5 cm) apart.

Bake until the cookies are shiny on top and dark golden brown, about 15 minutes. Transfer the cookies to wire racks and let cool completely.

Transfer the cream cheese frosting to a clean pastry bag fitted with a ¼-inch (6-mm) tip and pipe about 2 tablespoons of frosting onto the flat side of half of the cooled cookies. (Alternatively, use a zippered plastic bag or disposable pastry bag and cut off the tip of the bag to make a ¼-inch [6-mm] opening.) Top each with a second cookie, flat side down, and press together to spread the frosting to the edge.

caramelized pear ginger cake

Delicately perfumed pears partner flawlessly with spices like ginger, cardamom, and cinnamon, and they make a grand presentation in this caramelized upside-down cake. Make sure to invert the cake while it's still warm so that the caramel and pears don't stick. Serve this with lightly sweetened whipped crème fraîche if you like.

½ cup (4 oz/115 g) unsalted butter, at cool room temperature

½ cup (3½ oz/100 g) granulated sugar

2 ripe but firm large pears, such as Cornice or Anjou, peeled, cored, and cut lengthwise into ⅛-inch (3-mm) slices

1¾ cups (7½ oz/210 g) all-purpose flour

1½ teaspoons baking soda

2 teaspoons ground ginger

½ teaspoon ground cardamom

½ teaspoon ground cinnamon

¼ teaspoon salt

1 tablespoon peeled and finely chopped fresh ginger

⅓ cup (2¾ oz/80 g) firmly packed dark brown sugar

1 large egg

¾ cup (9 oz/240 g) light molasses

¾ cup (180 ml) whole milk, at room temperature

MAKES 9 SERVINGS

In a 9-inch (23-cm) cast-iron pan over medium heat, melt 2 tablespoons of the butter. Add the granulated sugar and cook, stirring occasionally, until the sugar melts and turns light brown, 5–7 minutes. Remove from the heat and arrange the pear slices in the pan in 4 overlapping rows. Set aside.

Preheat the oven to 350°F (180°C). Sift the flour, baking soda, ground ginger, cardamom, cinnamon, and salt together onto a sheet of waxed paper. Stir in the fresh ginger. Set aside.

In a bowl, using an electric mixer on medium speed, beat the remaining 6 tablespoons butter and brown sugar until fluffy, about 3–4 minutes. Add the egg and beat until well incorporated. Beat in the molasses. Reduce the speed to medium-low and add the flour mixture in 3 additions, alternating with the milk in 2 additions, and beginning and ending with the flour mixture. Beat just until combined.

Pour the batter over the pears and spread evenly to the edge of the pan. Bake until the top of the cake is puffed, 35–40 minutes. Transfer the pan to a wire rack and let cool for 5 minutes.

Run a table knife around the edge of the pan. Shake the pan to make sure the cake is not sticking. Place a serving plate upside down on the pan. Wearing oven mitts, invert the plate and pan together. Lift off the pan. Dislodge any pear slices that stick to the pan and arrange on top of the cake. Serve warm or at room temperature.

oatmeal pear crisp

This seasonal pear crisp relies on both rolled oats and oat bran, plus a hint of cardamom, for a memorable topping. Choose ripe but slightly firm pears that are also fragrant. Good baking varieties include Bartlett and Bosc. Enjoy this dessert warm with whipped cream or vanilla ice cream.

5 ripe but firm pears, peeled, cored, and sliced

3 tablespoons granulated sugar

2 tablespoons fresh lemon juice

½ cup (3½ oz/100 g) firmly packed light brown sugar

1 cup (3½ oz/100 g) rolled oats

¼ cup (1 oz/25 g) oat bran

⅔ cup (3 oz/80 g) all-purpose flour

1 teaspoon baking powder

½ teaspoon ground cardamom

6 tablespoons (3 oz/90 g) unsalted butter, cut into small pieces

1 recipe Whipped Cream (page 176), for serving

MAKES 6 SERVINGS

Preheat the oven to 350°F (180°C). Place the pear slices in a bowl. Sprinkle with the granulated sugar and toss gently. Spread the slices in an even layer in a shallow baking dish 12 inches (30 cm) in diameter. Sprinkle with the lemon juice.

In a bowl, stir together the brown sugar, oats, oat bran, flour, baking powder, and cardamom. Add the butter and rub into the oat mixture with your fingertips until the mixture is crumbly. Sprinkle evenly over the fruit. Bake until golden and crisp, about 40 minutes. Serve hot or warm, topped with a big dollop of whipped cream.

pistachio brittle

Nutty brittle is a crunchy, buttery confection that is most often made with peanuts, but this version swaps in pistachios for an entirely new flavor. Brittle, like chocolate bark and other homemade candies, makes a great gift during the holidays, plus it keeps for weeks in airtight parchment-lined containers. It's quick to make, so be sure you have all of your ingredients and kitchen tools at the ready.

1½ teaspoons baking soda

1 teaspoon vanilla extract

1½ cups (10½ oz/300 g) sugar

1 cup (11½ oz/325 g) light corn syrup

3 tablespoons unsalted butter, plus more for greasing

4 cups (1 lb/460 g) roasted, salted pistachios

**MAKES ABOUT
2 LB (1 KG) BRITTLE**

Preheat the oven to 250°F (120°C). Generously grease 2 rimmed baking sheets with unsalted butter and place in the oven.

In a small bowl, stir together the baking soda, vanilla, and 1 teaspoon water.

In a large, heavy saucepan over medium heat, cook the sugar, corn syrup, and 1 cup (240 ml) water, stirring just until the sugar is dissolved and the mixture is clear and registers 240°F (115°C) on a candy thermometer, 4–5 minutes. Stir in the butter and pistachios and cook, stirring constantly, until the mixture has thickened and registers 300°F (150°C) on a candy thermometer. Watch carefully to prevent the mixture from burning. Remove from the heat and immediately stir in the baking soda mixture. Be careful, as the mixture will bubble up.

Remove the baking sheets from the oven. Working quickly, carefully pour half of the candy mixture onto each warm baking sheet and spread it into an even layer about ¼ inch (6 mm) thick. Set aside to cool for about 1 hour. Lift the edge of the brittle and break it into large or small pieces.

maple pumpkin pie

For many, Thanksgiving just isn't the same without a big slice of homemade pumpkin pie topped with a dollop of whipped cream to end the meal. Using brown sugar and maple syrup highlights the flavors of the pumpkin and spices. This recipe makes use of canned pumpkin to keep things easy on a hectic holiday. If you like, substitute 1½ teaspoons pumpkin pie spice for the cinnamon, ginger, and nutmeg.

1 recipe Flaky Pie Dough, Single Crust (page 166)

2 tablespoons all-purpose flour, plus more for dusting

1 can (15-oz) pumpkin purée (about 1½ cups)

½ cup (3½ oz/100 g) firmly packed light brown sugar

½ cup (5½ oz/155 g) maple syrup

¾ cup (180 ml) whole milk

½ cup (125 ml) heavy cream

2 large eggs, lightly beaten

1 teaspoon ground cinnamon

¼ teaspoon ground ginger

⅛ teaspoon freshly grated nutmeg

¼ teaspoon salt

1 recipe Whipped Cream (page 176), for serving

MAKES 8 SERVINGS

Prepare the dough and chill as directed. On a lightly floured work surface roll out the dough into a round at least 12 inches (30 cm) in diameter and about ⅛ inch (3 mm) thick. Transfer to a 9-inch (23-cm) pie pan and ease into the pan. Trim the overhang to 1 inch (2.5 cm), fold the edge of the dough under itself to create a rim, and crimp the edges to seal. Prick the bottom of the crust all over with a fork and freeze for 30 minutes.

Preheat the oven to 400°F (200°C). Line the pie shell with aluminum foil and fill with pie weights or dried beans. Bake until the dough starts to look dry, about 15 minutes. Remove the foil and weights and continue to bake until the crust is just barely golden, about 5 minutes longer. Transfer to a wire rack and let cool completely. Reduce the oven temperature to 350°F (180°C).

In a large bowl, whisk together the pumpkin, brown sugar, and maple syrup. Add the milk, cream, and eggs and whisk to combine. Sift the flour, cinnamon, ginger, nutmeg, and salt over the pumpkin mixture and whisk to combine. Place the pie pan on a baking sheet. Pour the filling into the shell. Bake until the filling is just set and still jiggles very slightly in the center, about 1 hour. Transfer the dish to a wire rack and let cool for at least 1 hour to set.

Serve wedges of the pie with big spoonfuls of whipped cream.

caramel cranberry-almond tart

Here, creamy caramel is paired with fresh tart cranberries and toasty almonds for a balanced dessert. For the most flavor, cook the caramel until it is a deep golden brown, but be careful not to let it get overly dark, as it can easily burn. Once removed from the heat, the caramel thickens quickly so use it as soon as possible and re-melt it over low heat if necessary.

1 recipe Tart Dough
(page 167)

1 cup (7 oz/200 g) sugar

1 teaspoon light corn syrup

1 cup (250 ml) heavy cream

1½ cups (5¼ oz/150 g)
fresh or frozen cranberries

1 cup (3 oz/90 g) sliced
almonds, lightly toasted
(page 74)

MAKES 8 SERVINGS

Prepare the dough and chill as directed. On a lightly floured work surface, roll out the dough into a round at least 12 inches (30 cm) in diameter and about ⅛ inch (3 mm) thick. Transfer to a 9½-inch (24-cm) tart pan with a removable bottom and ease into the pan, patting it firmly into the bottom and up the sides of the pan. Trim off any excess dough by running a rolling pin across the top of the pan. Press the dough into the sides to extend it slightly above the rim. Prick the bottom of the tart shell all over with a fork. Refrigerate or freeze until firm, about 30 minutes.

Place a rack in the lower third of the oven and preheat to 375°F (190°C). Line the tart shell with aluminum foil and fill with pie weights or dried beans. Bake until the dough starts to look dry, about 15 minutes. Remove the foil and weights and continue to bake until the crust is just barely golden, about 5 minutes longer. Transfer to a wire rack and let cool completely. Reduce the oven temperature to 325°F (165°C).

In a saucepan over medium heat, stir together the sugar, 2 tablespoons water, and the corn syrup. Bring the mixture to a boil, shaking or tilting the pan but not stirring (which would cause the sugar to recrystallize), until the sugar dissolves and begins to turn golden. Reduce the heat to medium-low and continue cooking until the caramel becomes a deep golden brown, 6–8 minutes. Remove from the heat.

Slowly pour in the cream, being careful not to let the hot caramel bubble up and splatter. When the bubbling stops, whisk well. Add the cranberries and almonds and stir to combine. Pour the mixture into the partially baked tart shell and spread into an even layer.

Bake the tart until the cranberries have collapsed and the mixture is bubbling, 25–30 minutes. Transfer the pan to a wire rack and let cool completely. If using a tart pan with a removable bottom, let the sides fall away, then slide the tart onto a serving plate. Serve at room temperature.

chocolate, cherry & hazelnut biscotti

Crunchy biscotti are made for dunking into hot chocolate or coffee. The thick, flavorful cookies are twice-baked: First the dough is baked as a long log and then it's sliced and the cookies are toasted in the oven until crisp and dry. To dip biscotti in chocolate, melt 1 cup (6 oz/170 g) chocolate chips then dunk the bottoms or half of the biscotti in the chocolate. Let set on a wire rack.

1¾ cups (7½ oz/210 g) all-purpose flour, plus more for dusting

½ cup (1½ oz/40 g) unsweetened Dutch-process cocoa powder, sifted

1 cup (7 oz/200 g) granulated sugar

¼ cup (2 oz/60 g) firmly packed light brown sugar

1½ teaspoons baking powder

¼ teaspoon baking soda

¼ teaspoon salt

¾ cup (3¾ oz/105 g) dried tart cherries, coarsely chopped

¾ cup (3¾ oz/105 g) whole toasted hazelnuts (page 74), coarsely chopped

3 large eggs, plus 1 large egg white

1 teaspoon vanilla extract

MAKES ABOUT 48 BISCOTTI

Place 1 rack in the upper third and 1 rack in the lower third of the oven and preheat to 325°F (165°C). Line 2 baking sheets with parchment paper.

In a large bowl, sift together the flour, cocoa, granulated sugar, brown sugar, baking powder, baking soda, and salt. Add the cherries and hazelnuts and toss with your hands to distribute evenly.

In another bowl, whisk together the eggs, egg white, and vanilla. Pour the mixture into the flour mixture and mix with a fork, working the dry ingredients into the dough. This will take about 5 minutes. The dough will be dense and sticky.

Turn the dough out onto a floured work surface and divide in half. Transfer half the dough to a piece of plastic wrap 18 inches (45 cm) long. Lightly moisten your hands with cold water and shape the dough into a flattened log 12 inches (30 cm) long by 2½ inches (6 cm) wide by 1 inch (2.5 cm) high. Lifting the dough with the plastic wrap, flip the log onto the center of one of the prepared baking sheets. Repeat with the remaining half, flipping it onto the second prepared baking sheet.

Bake until the logs are dry to the touch and firm in the center, about 30 minutes. They will spread and may crack on top. Transfer the baking sheets to wire racks and let the logs cool for 30 minutes.

Transfer the logs to a cutting board. Using a serrated knife, cut the logs crosswise on the diagonal into slices ½ inch (12 mm) wide. Arrange the slices, cut side down, on the lined baking sheets, placing them close together but not touching. Return the baking sheets to the oven and bake for 15 minutes. Remove the baking sheets from the oven and turn over the biscotti slices. Continue to bake until the biscotti are dry and crisp, 10–15 minutes longer. Transfer the biscotti to wire racks to cool completely.

classic pecan pie

Sweet nutty pecans are harvested in late fall in the American South. Like most nuts, they are best stored for up to a month in the refrigerator or up to a year in the freezer. This old-fashioned pie needs no modern embellishments. Once baked, the pecans float to the surface, covering the pie with a wonderfully crunchy topping and leaving a rich, gooey layer underneath.

1 recipe Flaky Pie Dough, Single Crust (page 166)

3 large eggs

½ cup (3½ oz/100 g) sugar

1 cup (11½ oz/325 g) dark corn syrup

1 teaspoon vanilla extract

¼ teaspoon salt

¼ cup (2 oz/60 g) unsalted butter, melted

1½ cups (340 g) pecan halves, roughly chopped

1 recipe Whipped Cream (page 176), for serving

MAKES 8 SERVINGS

Prepare the dough and chill as directed. On a lightly floured work surface, roll out the dough into a round at least 12 inches (30 cm) in diameter and about ⅛ inch (3 mm) thick. Transfer to a 9-inch (23-cm) pie pan and ease into the pan. Trim the overhang to 1 inch (2.5 cm), fold the edge of the dough under itself to create a rim, and crimp the edges to seal. Prick the bottom of the crust all over with a fork and freeze for 30 minutes.

Preheat the oven to 400°F (200°C). Line the pie shell with aluminum foil and fill with pie weights or dried beans. Bake until the dough starts to look dry, about 15 minutes. Remove the foil and weights and continue to bake until the crust is just barely golden, about 5 minutes longer. Transfer the pan to a wire rack and let cool completely.

In a large bowl, whisk together the eggs, sugar, corn syrup, vanilla, and salt until blended, then whisk in the butter. Stir in the pecans. Pour the filling into the prebaked crust.

Bake until the filling is set but the center still jiggles slightly, 45–50 minutes. Transfer the pan to a wire rack and let cool. Serve warm or at room temperature, topped with whipped cream.

white chocolate grasshopper pie

Light and airy, this no-bake mousse pie has a subtle hint of mint from the crème de menthe liqueur that is folded into a white chocolate cream. A chocolate crumb crust, which can be homemade or purchased, plus plenty of chocolate shavings, are nice partners to the mint flavor. Be sure to include the layer of whipped cream for this spectacular adults-only dessert.

¼ cup (60 ml) crème de menthe

1 envelope unflavored gelatin

1½ cups (375 ml) heavy cream

2 oz (55 g) white chocolate, chopped

3 large egg yolks

⅓ cup (2½ oz/70 g) sugar

1 recipe Chocolate Wafer Cookie Crust (page 168), baked and cooled

1 recipe Whipped Cream (page 176)

Semisweet chocolate shavings, for garnish

MAKES 8 SERVINGS

Pour the crème de menthe into a small bowl and sprinkle the gelatin on top. Let stand until the gelatin softens and swells, about 5 minutes.

Pour ¾ cup (180 ml) of the cream into a heatproof bowl set over but not touching barely simmering water in a saucepan and stir gently until the cream is warm, then add the white chocolate and whisk until melted. Add the gelatin mixture and whisk until dissolved.

In a bowl, whisk together the egg yolks and sugar until blended. Slowly pour the hot cream mixture into the egg mixture, whisking constantly, then pour the mixture back into the bowl. Cook, whisking, until the mixture registers 150°F (65°C) on a candy thermometer, 3–5 minutes. Remove from the heat and let cool to room temperature.

In a bowl, using an electric mixer on high speed, beat the remaining ¾ cup (180 ml) cream until soft peaks form. Fold the whipped cream into the white chocolate mixture, then pour the filling into the crust. Refrigerate for at least 2 hours or up to overnight.

To serve, top the pie with whipped cream and garnish with chocolate shavings.

apple-ginger tart with cider-bourbon sauce

A terrific addition to a holiday gathering, especially when you want something a little more upscale than a classic apple pie, this streusel-topped tart is served with a boozy, buttery bourbon sauce. A single dough creates the crust and crumbly topping. Both the tart and sauce can be made earlier in the day and reheated in a low oven just before serving.

FOR THE CRUMB CRUST

1¼ cups (5½ oz/155 g)
all-purpose flour

⅔ cup (5 oz/140 g)
cold unsalted butter

2 tablespoons
confectioners' sugar

FOR THE FILLING

⅓ cup (2¾ oz/80 g) firmly
packed light brown sugar

2½ lb (1.25 kg) crisp-tart
baking apples, such as Granny
Smith, Honeycrisp, or Gala,
cored and thinly sliced

¼ cup (1¾ oz/50 g)
granulated sugar

3 tablespoons fresh
lemon juice

⅓ cup (2 oz/55 g) finely
chopped crystallized ginger

1 teaspoon ground cinnamon

FOR THE SAUCE

1 cup (7½ oz/210 g) firmly
packed light brown sugar

2 tablespoons cornstarch

2 cups (500 ml) apple cider

Pinch of salt

¼ cup (2 oz/60 g) unsalted
butter, cut into pieces

½ cup (120 ml) bourbon

MAKES 8 SERVINGS

To make the crumb crust, in a food processor, combine the flour, butter, and confectioners' sugar and pulse until fine crumbs form. Measure out ½ cup (115 g) of the crumb mixture and set aside. Press the remaining crumb mixture evenly in the bottom and up the sides of an 11-inch (28-cm) tart pan with a removable bottom. Refrigerate or freeze the tart shell for 10 minutes.

Preheat the oven to 425°F (220°C). Bake until the crust just begins to brown, about 6 minutes. Let cool on a wire rack while you make the filling.

To make the filling, in a small bowl, mix together the reserved crumb mixture and the brown sugar. In a large bowl, combine the apple slices, granulated sugar, lemon juice, ginger, and cinnamon and toss to coat the apples. Arrange the apple filling in the cooled pastry shell. Sprinkle with the crumb mixture.

Bake for 15 minutes, then reduce the oven temperature to 375°F (190°C) and bake until the apples are tender when pierced with a knife, 45–50 minutes longer. Cover the top with aluminum foil during the last 30 minutes to prevent the top from overbrowning. Transfer the pan to a wire rack and let cool.

To make the sauce, in a small saucepan over medium heat, combine the brown sugar and cornstarch, stirring to remove any lumps. Stir in the apple cider and salt. Raise the heat to medium-high and bring to a boil, stirring constantly. Cook until thickened, about 4 minutes. Reduce the heat to medium, stir in the butter and bourbon, and simmer just until well blended.

Cut the tart into wedges. Drizzle a little of the hot cider–bourbon sauce over each wedge, and serve.

honey-nut pie

With loads of mixed nuts, plus a surprise layer of chocolate at the bottom, this candy bar–like pie is a nut-lover's fantasy! Choose any combination of your favorite nuts for this pie, just make sure they are untoasted and unsalted, as they will toast when baked. A sprinkle of flaky sea salt highlights the sweet, nutty flavor of the pie.

1 recipe Flaky Pie Dough, Single Crust (page 166)

6 oz (170 g) semisweet chocolate, melted and cooled slightly

3 cups (about 1 lb/460 g) assorted raw unsalted nuts, such as almonds, pecans, macadamia nuts, hazelnuts, pistachios, peanuts, and/ or walnuts

½ cup (2¼ oz/65 g) pepitas

½ cup (3½ oz/100 g) sugar

⅓ cup (80 ml) heavy cream

¼ cup (2 oz/85 g) honey

¼ cup (3 oz/80 g) corn syrup

¼ cup (2 oz/60 g) unsalted butter, cut into cubes

1 teaspoon vanilla extract

Pinch of salt

Flaky sea salt, for sprinkling

MAKES 8 SERVINGS

Prepare the dough and chill as directed. On a lightly floured work surface, roll out the dough into a round at least 12 inches (30 cm) in diameter and about ⅛ inch (3 mm) thick. Transfer to a 9-inch (23-cm) pie pan and ease into the pan. Trim the overhang to 1 inch (2.5 cm), fold the edge of the dough under itself to create a rim, and crimp the edges to seal. Prick the bottom of the crust all over with a fork and freeze for 30 minutes.

Preheat the oven to 400°F (200°C). Line the pie shell with aluminum foil and fill with pie weights or dried beans. Bake until the dough starts to look dry, about 15 minutes. Remove the foil and weights and continue to bake until the crust is just barely golden, about 5 minutes longer. Transfer to a wire rack and let cool completely. Reduce the oven temperature to 350°F (180°C).

Spread the melted chocolate over the bottom of the crust and let cool to room temperature.

Spread the nuts and pepitas on a baking sheet. Toast in the oven until golden brown, about 10 minutes. Let cool.

In a saucepan over medium heat, combine the sugar, cream, honey, and corn syrup. Stir occasionally until the mixture is slightly thickened and coats the back of the spoon, 2–4 minutes. Remove from the heat. Add the butter, vanilla, and salt and stir until the butter is melted. Stir in the nuts and pepitas. Pour the filling into the crust. Sprinkle with the flaky salt.

Bake until the filling is set, about 30 minutes, covering the top with aluminum foil if the nuts brown too quickly. Transfer the pan to a wire rack and let cool for at least 4 hours or up to overnight before serving.

classic tarte tatin

Tarte tatin is a timeless bistro classic, with buttery caramelized apples atop flaky golden pastry. The technique might seem complicated, but as long as you flip the frying pan while the dessert is warm and keep the pan and plate together, your efforts will be rewarded. Choose crisp-tart apples that hold their shape when baked.

1 recipe Flaky Pie Dough, Single Crust (page 166)

¼ cup (2 oz/60 g) unsalted butter, cut into pieces

¾ cup (5 oz/140 g) sugar

5 crisp-tart apples, such as Pink Lady, Honeycrisp, or Gala, peeled, cored, and quartered lengthwise

Vanilla ice cream, for serving (optional)

MAKES 8 SERVINGS

Prepare the dough and chill as directed. On a lightly floured work surface, roll out the dough into a round about 11 inches (28 cm) in diameter and about ¼ inch (6 mm) thick. Cover the round with plastic wrap and refrigerate until ready to use.

Preheat the oven to 375°F (190°C).

Place a 10-inch (25-cm) straight-sided, ovenproof frying pan, preferably cast iron, over medium heat and warm the butter. When it melts, sprinkle the sugar evenly over the butter and continue cooking until the sugar melts and turns amber colored, 3–4 minutes. Swirl the pan frequently to redistribute the sugar. Arrange the apples, core side up, in the caramel in a snug even layer. Raise the heat to medium-high and cook until the apples are just tender, about 15 minutes. The caramel will bubble up around the apples. Remove the pan from the heat.

When the bubbling has subsided, slide both hands under the dough round and carefully place it on top of the apples, tucking in the edges and being careful not to burn your fingers. Bake until the crust is golden brown, about 30 minutes. Transfer the pan to a wire rack and let cool for 5 minutes. Place a large flat plate upside down on the pan and invert the pan and plate together. Lift off the pan. Serve warm with vanilla ice cream, if you like.

butterscotch-bourbon pie

Caramelized brown sugar custard pie with hints of vanilla and bourbon is a natural in the fall and would be at home on any holiday buffet. Use a decent-quality bourbon in the pie and then serve small drams of it alongside.

1 recipe Flaky Pie Dough, Single Crust (page 166)

1½ cups (375 ml) whole milk

1½ cups (375 ml) heavy cream

1 vanilla bean, split, with seeds scraped, seeds and pod reserved

¼ cup (2 oz/60 g) unsalted butter

¾ cup (5½ oz/155 g) firmly packed dark brown sugar

9 large egg yolks

3 tablespoons cornstarch

½ teaspoon salt

2 tablespoons bourbon

1 teaspoon fresh lemon juice

1 recipe Whipped Cream (page 176), for serving

MAKES 8 SERVINGS

Prepare the dough and chill as directed. On a lightly floured work surface, roll out the dough into a round at least 12 inches (30 cm) in diameter and about ⅛ inch (3 mm) thick. Transfer to a 9-inch (23-cm) pie pan and ease into the pan. Trim the overhang to 1 inch (2.5 cm), fold the edge of the dough under itself to create a rim, and crimp the edges to seal. Prick the bottom of the crust all over with a fork and freeze for 30 minutes.

Preheat the oven to 400°F (200°C). Line the pie shell with aluminum foil and fill with pie weights or dried beans. Bake until the dough starts to look dry, about 15 minutes. Remove the foil and weights and continue to bake until the crust is just barely golden, about 5 minutes longer. Transfer to a wire rack and let cool completely. Reduce the oven temperature to 350°F (180°C).

In a small saucepan over medium heat, combine the milk, cream, and vanilla bean seeds and pod and bring to a gentle simmer. Remove from the heat and let stand for 5 minutes. Discard the vanilla pod.

In a large saucepan over medium heat, melt the butter. Reduce the heat to low and cook until golden with a nutty fragrance, about 6 minutes. Stir in half of the brown sugar and the milk mixture. Remove from the heat.

In a large bowl, whisk together the egg yolks, cornstarch, salt, and the remaining brown sugar until well blended. Add the hot milk mixture, ¼ cup (60 ml) at a time, to the egg yolk mixture, whisking constantly, then pour the mixture back into the pan. Stir constantly over medium–high heat until the mixture boils. Reduce the heat to medium and stir constantly until the mixture is thick enough to coat the spoon, 6–8 minutes. Stir in the bourbon and lemon juice. Pour the mixture through a fine-mesh sieve into the crust.

Bake until the edges of the pie are set but the center still jiggles slightly, 25–35 minutes, covering the edges with aluminum foil if they brown too quickly. Let cool completely on a wire rack. Serve at room temperature or chilled up to overnight, topped with whipped cream.

almond-jam cakes

You'd never know that these delicate, tender almond cakes are gluten-free, but they are! Both almond flour and almond paste contribute to the nutty flavor. The hint of lemon is a nice partner to the dollop of raspberry jam that sits atop each cake. Dust the cakes with confectioners' sugar just before serving for a beautiful presentation.

1¼ cups (4 oz/120 g) almond flour

½ cup (2 oz/60 g) cornstarch

2 teaspoons baking powder

7 oz (210 g) almond paste

⅔ cup (4¾ oz/140 g) granulated sugar

Grated zest of 1 lemon

½ teaspoon salt

¾ cup (6 oz/170 g) unsalted butter, melted and cooled

4 large eggs, at room temperature

⅓ cup (3 oz/95 g) raspberry jam

Confectioners' sugar for dusting

MAKES 16 MINI CAKES

Preheat the oven to 350°F (180°C). Spray 16 standard muffin cups with nonstick cooking spray.

In a bowl, mix together the almond flour, cornstarch, and baking powder.

Using the small holes on a box grater-shredder, grate the almond paste into a large bowl. Add the sugar, lemon zest, and salt to the almond paste and, using an electric mixer on medium-low speed, beat until the almond paste breaks up and looks like bread crumbs, about 2 minutes. Raise the speed to medium-high, add the butter, and beat until smooth, about 2 minutes. Add the eggs one at a time, beating well and stopping the mixer and scraping down the sides of the bowl after each addition. Raise the speed to high and beat until the mixture is fully blended, about 1 minute. Reduce the speed to low, add the almond flour mixture, and beat just until combined.

Divide the batter among the prepared muffin cups, filling them about three-fourths full. Bake until golden brown and a toothpick inserted into the center of a cake comes out clean, about 18 minutes. Transfer the pans to wire racks and let cool for about 10 minutes, then invert the cakes onto the racks and turn them right side up. Spoon about 1 teaspoon of the jam onto the center of each cake, smoothing it into a round. Let the cakes cool completely.

Just before serving, using a small fine-mesh sieve, dust each cake with confectioners' sugar.

pumpkin chocolate chip cupcakes

These spiced pumpkin and chocolate chip cupcakes are perfect for Halloween. Chocolate and vanilla glazes are used to create a simple yet spooky spiderweb design—and all you need is a toothpick to create the pattern. For an everyday version of these cupcakes, simply spread the cupcakes with either the chocolate or vanilla glaze or leave it off altogether.

1 cup (4¼ oz/120 g)
all-purpose flour

1 teaspoon baking powder

½ teaspoon baking soda

¼ teaspoon salt

2 teaspoons pumpkin
pie spice

1 cup (8 oz/225 g) canned
pumpkin purée

1 cup (7 oz/200 g) sugar

½ cup (125 ml) avocado
or canola oil

2 large eggs

1 cup (6 oz/170 g) mini
semisweet chocolate chips

1 recipe Chocolate
Glaze (page 155)

1 recipe Vanilla Glaze
(page 155)

MAKES 12 CUPCAKES

Preheat the oven to 350°F (180°C). Line 12 standard muffin cups with paper liners.

In a small bowl, whisk together the flour, baking powder, baking soda, salt, and pumpkin pie spice. In a large bowl, whisk together the pumpkin purée, sugar, oil, and eggs. Add the flour mixture and whisk until well combined. Using a rubber spatula, fold in the chocolate chips.

Divide the batter evenly among the prepared muffin cups. Bake until a toothpick inserted into the center of a cupcake comes out clean, 22–24 minutes. Transfer the pan to a wire rack and let cool for 10 minutes. Remove the cupcakes from the pan and let cool completely on the rack, about 1 hour.

Spoon the chocolate glaze over the cupcakes. To make spiderweb designs, fit a small pastry bag with a small plain tip, then transfer the vanilla glaze to the bag. Pipe concentric circles of vanilla glaze onto a chocolate-glazed cupcake. Lightly draw the tip of a toothpick or wooden skewer from the center of the cupcake outward to the edge, spacing the lines evenly and occasionally alternating the direction. For the cleanest look, wipe the tip of the toothpick or skewer after each draw. Repeat with the remaining cupcakes. Let the glaze dry for about 30 minutes before serving.

devil's food chocolate cupcakes

Devil's food cake is so named for its deep rich color and flavor. The secret to this cake is mixing natural cocoa powder, not Dutch-process cocoa, with boiling water, which allows the flavor to bloom and adds moisture to the cake. For a two-layer cake, divide the batter between two 9-inch (23-cm) round cake pans and add a few minutes to the baking time.

1 cup (240 ml) boiling water

¾ cup (2¼ oz/60 g) unsweetened cocoa powder

1¾ cups (7½ oz/210 g) all-purpose flour

1½ teaspoons baking soda

¼ teaspoon salt

1½ cups (10½ oz/300 g) sugar

¼ cup (5 oz/140 g) unsalted butter, at cool room temperature

3 large eggs

1 teaspoon vanilla extract

1¼ cups (310 ml) buttermilk

2 recipes Chocolate Frosting (page 172)

Sprinkles, for decorating (optional)

MAKES 18 CUPCAKES

Preheat the oven to 350°F (180°C). Line 18 cups of two standard muffin pans with paper liners.

In a small heatproof bowl, whisk together the boiling water and cocoa until smooth. Let cool completely.

In a bowl, sift together the flour, baking soda, and salt. In a large bowl, using an electric mixer on medium-high speed, beat together the sugar and butter until the mixture is light in color and texture, about 3 minutes. Beat in the eggs, one at a time, then beat in the vanilla and the cooled cocoa mixture. Reduce the speed to low and add the flour mixture in 3 additions, alternating with the buttermilk and beginning and ending with the flour, and stopping to scrape down the bowl as needed, beating until smooth. Divide the batter among the prepared cups, filling them about three-fourths full.

Bake until the tops spring back when pressed in the center, 20–25 minutes. Remove the cupcakes from the pans and let cool completely on the rack, about 30 minutes.

Transfer the frosting to a piping bag fitted with a large star tip and frost the cupcakes. Decorate with sprinkles, if you like, and serve.

bread & butter pudding with marmalade

Soft and custardy on the inside, with a crisp, jammy crust, this British version of bread pudding is a great way to use up stale bread. The difference lies in spreading the slices of bread with plenty of softened butter, adding to the richness of the dessert. This version uses eggy challah or brioche, but you can also use spiced rolls or soft-crusted French bread.

3 tablespoons unsalted butter, at cool room temperature, plus more for greasing

1 (1-lb/450-g) loaf challah or brioche, ends trimmed and cut into 12 slices

3 large eggs plus 5 large egg yolks

1¾ cups (430 ml) whole milk

1 cup (250 ml) heavy cream

⅓ cup (2½ oz/70 g) sugar

1 teaspoon vanilla extract

¼ teaspoon salt

¼ teaspoon ground cinnamon

⅛ teaspoon freshly grated nutmeg

½ cup (5 oz/155 g) orange marmalade

1 recipe Whipped Cream (page 176) for serving

MAKES 8 SERVINGS

Preheat the oven to 325°F (165°C). Generously grease a 9-by-13-inch (23-by-33-cm) baking dish. Spread the challah slices thickly and evenly with the butter. Cut the slices in half crosswise. Lay the slices in the dish so that they overlap slightly.

In a bowl, whisk together the eggs, egg yolks, milk, cream, sugar, vanilla, salt, cinnamon, and nutmeg. Pour the mixture evenly over the bread. Let stand for about 30 minutes so that the bread soaks up the custard, occasionally pressing down on the bread.

Bake the pudding for 30 minutes. Meanwhile, in a small saucepan over medium-low heat, gently warm the marmalade. Remove the pudding from the oven and carefully spread the marmalade over the top. Return to the oven and bake until the top is crisp, brown, and sticky, about 10 minutes longer. Let stand for about 10 minutes before serving big scoops of the pudding topped with the whipped cream.

sweet potato corn bread

The orange-golden color of this corn bread roots it squarely in autumn, when root vegetables are in abundance. Be sure to use orange-fleshed sweet potatoes, sometimes called yams, as they are sweeter and silkier than the yellow varieties. Serve slices of this corn bread warm with salted butter, drizzled with honey for a special treat.

1 lb (450 g) orange-fleshed sweet potatoes, peeled and cut into chunks

1 cup (130 g) fine-grind cornmeal

1 cup (4¼ oz/120 g) all-purpose flour

1 tablespoon sugar

1 tablespoon baking powder

½ teaspoon baking soda

½ teaspoon salt

⅛ teaspoon ground cinnamon

1¼ cups (310 ml) buttermilk

2 large eggs, lightly beaten

3 tablespoons unsalted butter, melted

MAKES ONE 9-INCH (23-CM) CORN BREAD

Bring a saucepan three-fourths full of water to a boil over high heat, add the sweet potatoes, and cook until tender, 15–20 minutes. Remove from the heat and drain thoroughly. Transfer to a food processor and process to a smooth purée. Scrape into a bowl and let cool to room temperature.

Preheat the oven to 400°F (200°C). Grease a 9-inch (23-cm) square baking pan with nonstick cooking spray.

In a small bowl, whisk together the cornmeal, flour, sugar, baking powder, baking soda, salt, and cinnamon.

Add the buttermilk, eggs, and melted butter to the sweet potatoes and mix well. Add the cornmeal mixture and stir just until combined, taking care not to overmix. The batter should be slightly lumpy. Pour the batter into the prepared pan.

Bake until the top is golden brown and the bread pulls away from the pan sides, 30–35 minutes. Transfer the pan to a wire rack to cool slightly or completely. Cut into squares to serve.

cranberry upside-down cake

The moment you invert an upside-down cake and reveal the caramelized glistening fruit hiding at the bottom of the pan is something magical. Cranberries create a bright sweet-tart layer on top of a simple sour cream–based cake. Be sure to line the pan with parchment paper to prevent the berries and glaze from sticking when you flip the pan over.

¼ cup (2 oz/60 g) unsalted butter, plus more for greasing

¾ cup (5½ oz/155 g) firmly packed light brown sugar

2 cups (7 oz/200 g) fresh or thawed frozen cranberries

1¼ cups (5½ oz/155 g) all-purpose flour

½ teaspoon baking powder

¼ teaspoon baking soda

¼ teaspoon salt

1 large egg

1 cup (7 oz/200 g) granulated sugar

½ cup (125 ml) avocado or canola oil

1 teaspoon vanilla extract

½ cup (4 oz/115 g) sour cream

1 recipe Whipped Cream (page 176), for serving (optional)

MAKES 8–10 SERVINGS

Preheat the oven to 350°F (180°C). Grease a 9-inch (23-cm) round cake pan, line the bottom of the pan with parchment paper, then butter the parchment.

In a small saucepan over medium-low heat, combine the butter and brown sugar. Cook, stirring, until the butter is melted and the mixture is smooth. Carefully scrape the glaze into the prepared pan, tilting the pan to spread it evenly. Arrange the cranberries evenly over the glaze.

In a medium bowl, sift together the flour, baking powder, baking soda, and salt. In a large bowl, using an electric mixer on medium speed, beat the egg and granulated sugar until light and fluffy, about 2 minutes. Stop the mixer and scrape down the sides of the bowl. Reduce the speed to low, slowly add the oil and vanilla, and beat until blended. Mix in the sour cream just until no white streaks remain. Add the flour mixture and mix on low speed until incorporated. Pour the batter over the cranberries, spreading it evenly.

Bake until a wooden skewer inserted into the center of the cake comes out clean, about 45 minutes. Remove the pan from the oven and let cool on a wire rack for 5 minutes. Run a table knife around the inside edge of the pan. Place a plate upside down on top of the pan and turn the pan and plate over together to unmold the cake. Lift off the pan and carefully peel off the parchment paper. Cut the cake into wedges. Serve with whipped cream, if you like.

pumpkin coffee cake with pecan streusel

There's something wonderful about old-fashioned coffee cake, and this recipe is surely something special. This spiced cake is lighter than you might expect, with a thick layer of toasted pecan and brown sugar streusel that makes it ideal for a festive autumn brunch.

FOR THE PECAN STREUSEL

1 cup (4¼ oz/120 g)
all-purpose flour

⅔ cup (5 oz/140 g) firmly
packed light brown sugar

1 teaspoon ground cinnamon

⅛ teaspoon salt

⅓ cup (3 oz/90 g) unsalted
butter, melted

1 cup (4 oz/115 g) chopped
pecans, toasted (page 74)

FOR THE COFFEE CAKE

1½ cups (6½ oz/180 g)
all-purpose flour

2 teaspoons baking powder

½ teaspoon baking soda

2 teaspoons ground cinnamon

1 teaspoon ground ginger

¼ teaspoon freshly
grated nutmeg

½ teaspoon salt

½ cup (4 oz/115 g) unsalted
butter, plus more for greasing

1 cup (7⅓ oz/210 g) firmly
packed light brown sugar

2 large eggs

½ cup (4 oz/55 g)
pumpkin purée

½ cup (4 oz/115 g) sour cream

½ recipe Vanilla Icing
(page 170)

MAKES 8–12 SERVINGS

Preheat the oven to 350°F (180°C). Grease a 9-inch (23-cm) springform pan or a 9-by-3-inch (23-by-7.5-cm) cake pan with butter. Dust with flour, then tap out any excess.

To make the streusel, in a bowl, combine the flour, brown sugar, cinnamon, and salt. Add the butter and, using a fork, stir it into the flour mixture until the mixture looks like coarse crumbs. Stir in the pecans.

To make the coffee cake, in a bowl, sift together the flour, baking powder, baking soda, cinnamon, ginger, nutmeg, and salt. In a bowl, using an electric mixer on medium-high speed, beat the butter and brown sugar until well combined. Beat in the eggs, one at a time, scraping down the sides of the bowl as needed. Add the pumpkin purée and sour cream and mix until combined. Reduce the speed to low, add the flour mixture, and beat until combined. The batter will be quite thick.

Spread half of the batter in the prepared pan. Sprinkle half of the streusel over the batter. Dollop the remaining batter over the streusel and spread the batter into an even layer. Top with the remaining streusel.

Bake until a toothpick inserted into the center of the cake comes out clean, about 50 minutes. Transfer the pan to a wire rack and let cool for about 15 minutes. Remove the sides from the pan and slide the cake onto the rack.

Drizzle the icing over the top of the coffee cake. Cut into thick wedges and serve.

challah

Plump braided challah is a tender, eggy yeast bread that is traditionally served on the Jewish Sabbath. It can be braided using three or more strands. The addition of saffron gives the bread a deeper golden hue, but you can leave it out if you like.

About 5 cups (21¼ oz/620 g) all-purpose flour, plus more for dusting

¼ cup (1¾ oz/50 g) sugar

1 tablespoon active dry yeast

1¼ cups (300 ml) warm water (110°F/43°C)

6 tablespoons (3 oz/90 g) unsalted butter, at cool room temperature, plus more for greasing

3 large eggs

1 tablespoon salt

⅛ teaspoon powdered saffron (optional)

1 tablespoon whole milk

1 tablespoon sesame seeds or poppy seeds (optional)

MAKES 1 LARGE LOAF

In the bowl of a stand mixer fitted with the dough hook, combine 1½ cups (6½ oz/180 g) of the flour, the sugar, and the yeast. Add the water and beat on medium-high speed just until well mixed. Let sit for 10 minutes until foamy. Beat in the butter and 2 of the eggs. Add 3 cups (12¾ oz/360 g) flour, the salt, and saffron, if using, to make a dough that is semisoft and no longer sticky. Add a little more flour if the dough is too wet.

Transfer the dough to a floured work surface and knead, adding flour as needed to prevent sticking, until smooth and elastic, about 5 minutes. Gather the dough into a ball, place in a large bowl greased with butter, turn to coat with the butter, and cover the bowl with a damp kitchen towel. Place in a warm, draft-free area until doubled in size, about 1½ hours.

Transfer the dough to a lightly floured work surface. Knead until smooth, about 3 minutes. Divide the dough into 3 equal portions. Using your palms, roll each portion into a rope 20 inches (50 cm) long.

Line a baking sheet with parchment paper. Braid the ropes together and transfer the braid to the prepared sheet, tucking the ends under themselves. Cover with the kitchen towel and let rise in a warm, draft-free area until doubled in size, about 1 hour.

Meanwhile, preheat the oven to 350°F (180°C). In a small bowl, beat the remaining egg with the milk until blended. Gently brush the egg wash evenly over the braid. Sprinkle with the sesame seeds, if using. Bake until the bread is golden brown and sounds hollow when thumped on the bottom, about 55 minutes. Let cool on a rack.

cinnamon rolls

Sticky, gooey cinnamon rolls are an event, whether you make them for a holiday breakfast or a lazy Sunday morning. And there's possibly no better aroma than that of these puffy rolls baking in the oven, fragrant with cinnamon and orange zest. If you like, add ⅓ cup (2 oz/60 g) raisins or toasted chopped pecans to the filling. Prepare the rolls the night before up until the final rise and baking. The next morning, let them come to room temperature for an hour, then bake and serve.

FOR THE DOUGH

1 package (2¼ teaspoons) active dry yeast

¾ cup (180 ml) warm whole milk (110°F/43°C)

¼ cup (1¾ oz/50 g) granulated sugar

4 large eggs

4½ cups (19 oz/540 g) all-purpose flour, plus more as needed

1 teaspoon salt

6 tablespoons (3 oz/90 g) unsalted butter, at cool room temperature, cut into chunks

FOR THE FILLING

⅔ cup (5 oz/140 g) firmly packed light brown sugar

2 teaspoons ground cinnamon

Finely grated zest of 1 orange

¼ cup (2 oz/60 g) unsalted butter, at cool room temperature, plus more for greasing

1 egg, lightly beaten with 1 teaspoon water

1 recipe Cream Cheese Frosting (page 173)

MAKES 16 ROLLS

To make the dough, in the bowl of a stand mixer, dissolve the yeast in the warm milk and let stand until foamy, about 10 minutes. Add the granulated sugar, eggs, flour, and salt. Attach the dough hook and knead on low speed, adding a little more flour if needed, until the ingredients come together. Sprinkle in the butter and continue to knead until the dough is smooth and springy, about 7 minutes. Lightly oil a large bowl. Form the dough into a ball, put it in the oiled bowl, and cover the bowl with plastic wrap. Let the dough rise at room temperature until it doubles, 1½–2 hours.

To make the filling, in a small bowl, whisk together the brown sugar, cinnamon, and orange zest.

Grease a 9-by-13-inch (23-by-33-cm) baking dish.

Punch down the dough. Turn the dough out onto a lightly floured work surface and divide in half. Roll out 1 dough half into a rectangle about 9 by 14 inches (23 by 35 cm). Spread with 2 tablespoons of the butter, then sprinkle evenly with half of the filling. Starting at the long side closest to you, roll the rectangle away from you, forming a log. Cut the log crosswise into 8 equal slices. Arrange the slices, cut side down, on half of the prepared dish. Repeat with the remaining dough and filling ingredients, and arrange the slices in the other half of the dish. Cover the dish loosely with plastic wrap and let stand in a warm, draft-free spot until puffy, about 1 hour, or refrigerate overnight, then let stand at room temperature for 1 hour before baking.

Preheat the oven to 400°F (200°C). Brush the buns lightly with the egg wash. Bake until the rolls are golden brown and a toothpick inserted into the center of a roll comes out clean, 20–25 minutes. Transfer the dish to a wire rack and let the rolls cool slightly, then spread with the frosting while they are still warm. Serve.

winter

meyer lemon curd pavlova with blood oranges & cream

Pavlova is a beloved dessert in Australia and New Zealand, with a base of crisp-chewy meringue topped with whipped cream and fruit. This pavlova makes use of winter citrus with the addition of lemon curd and marinated blood oranges. All of these elements can be made in advance, so it's a great dessert for entertaining. In summer, make this with fresh berries, sliced mango and kiwi, or ripe peaches.

FOR THE MARINATED BLOOD ORANGES

3 lb (1.4 kg) blood oranges

1 tablespoon fresh lemon juice

2 tablespoons sugar

⅓ cup (80 ml) Tuaca or orange liqueur

FOR THE MERINGUE

4 large egg whites

Pinch of salt

1 cup (7 oz/200 g) sugar

1 teaspoon cornstarch

½ teaspoon malt vinegar

1 recipe Meyer Lemon Curd (page 177)

1 recipe Whipped Cream (page 176), for serving

SERVES 8

To make the marinated blood oranges, using a sharp knife, slice off both ends of each orange to reveal the flesh. Place an orange upright on the cutting board and, following the contour of the fruit, cut downward to remove all of the peel and white pith. Cut into segments, then repeat. Repeat with the remaining oranges.

In a small bowl, stir together the lemon juice, sugar, and Tuaca. Pour the mixture over the orange segments and toss gently to combine. Cover and refrigerate until well chilled, at least 3 hours or up to 24 hours.

To make the meringue, preheat the oven to 325°F (165°C). Line a baking sheet with parchment paper. In a bowl, using an electric mixer on high speed, beat the egg whites and salt until foamy, about 2 minutes. Gradually beat in the sugar and continue to beat until stiff, glossy peaks form, about 3–5 minutes. Beat in the cornstarch and vinegar.

Spoon 8 dollops of the meringue onto the prepared baking sheet, dividing the mixture evenly and spacing them 1–2 inches (2.5–5 cm) apart, or, for 1 large meringue, spoon the mixture into a single large mound. Use the back of the spoon to create an indentation in the center of each mound.

Bake for 2 minutes, then reduce the oven temperature to 250°F (120°C). Continue to bake until the meringue is crisp to the touch, about 1 hour for individual meringues or 1 hour 40 minutes for a large meringue. Turn off the oven and leave the meringue(s) in the oven to cool completely, about 2 hours.

To serve, place the meringues on plate(s) and fill the center(s) with the curd, dividing it evenly. Top with whipped cream and the marinated blood oranges, then serve.

almond cookies

These almond-rich butter cookies are often served at Chinese New Year celebrations. They have a whole blanched or natural almond pressed into the center of each cookie before baking, but you can also use a sliced almond if you like. The egg wash gives each cookie a glistening shine.

½ cup (4 oz/115 g) unsalted butter, at cool room temperature

½ cup (3½ oz/100 g) sugar

¼ teaspoon salt

1 large egg

½ teaspoon almond extract

1 cup (4¼ oz/120 g) all-purpose flour

½ teaspoon baking soda

½ cup (1½ oz/50 g) almond flour

18–20 whole almonds

1 large egg, beaten with 1 teaspoon water

MAKES 18–20 COOKIES

In a large bowl, using an electric mixer on medium speed, beat together the butter, sugar, and salt until pale and fluffy, about 2 minutes. Add the egg and almond extract and beat until blended. Turn off the mixer and scrape down the sides of the bowl. Sift together the flour and baking soda over the butter mixture, then add the almond flour. Beat on low speed just until combined. Shape the dough into a ball, cover the bowl, and refrigerate for at least 1 hour or up to overnight.

Preheat the oven to 325°F (165°C). Line a baking sheet with parchment paper.

Scoop up a tablespoon of the chilled dough and roll it between your palms into a ball about 1 inch (2.5 cm) in diameter. Place on the prepared baking sheet. Repeat with the remaining dough, spacing the balls about 1½ inches (4 cm) apart. You should have 18–20 balls. Using your hand, flatten each ball to about ¼ inch (6 mm) thick. The cookies should be at least 1 inch (2.5 cm) apart. Place a whole almond in the center of each cookie. Brush each cookie lightly with the egg wash.

Bake until the cookies are golden, about 20 minutes. Transfer the cookies to a wire rack and let cool completely. The cookies are best eaten the day they are baked.

hot cocoa cookies

A steaming cup of hot chocolate with marshmallows on top is the perfect way to warm up after a day in the snow. These cookies take the flavor of hot cocoa and transform it into chewy cookies topped with toasty marshmallows. Making them is a great way to spend a stormy winter afternoon, and they would be a terrific addition to a holiday cookie platter.

1½ cups (6½ oz/180 g)
all-purpose flour

½ cup (1½ oz/40 g)
unsweetened cocoa powder,
plus more for dusting

¼ cup (20 g)
hot chocolate mix

1 teaspoon baking powder

¼ teaspoon salt

3 large eggs

1⅔ cups (11½ oz/325 g) sugar

2 teaspoons vanilla extract

¼ cup (2 oz/60 g)
unsalted butter, melted
and cooled slightly

13 jumbo marshmallows,
halved crosswise

MAKES ABOUT 26 COOKIES

In a bowl, whisk together the flour, cocoa powder, hot chocolate mix, baking powder, and salt. In a bowl, using an electric mixer on high speed, beat the eggs, sugar, and vanilla until light in color and thick, about 3 minutes. Reduce the speed to medium, add the butter, and beat until blended. Stop the mixer and scrape down the sides of the bowl. Add the flour mixture and mix on low speed just until blended. Cover the bowl with plastic wrap and refrigerate for 1 hour.

Place 1 rack in the upper third and 1 rack in the lower third of the oven and preheat to 350°F (180°C). Line 2 baking sheets with parchment paper.

Scoop up the chilled dough by heaping tablespoonfuls and roll into balls between the palms of your hands. Place the balls on the prepared baking sheets, spacing them 2 inches (5 cm) apart.

Bake for 6 minutes, then rotate the baking sheets between the racks. Continue to bake until the cookies are puffed and look dry, 4–6 minutes longer. Transfer the baking sheets to wire racks and let cool for 5 minutes, then transfer the cookies directly to the racks and let cool completely.

Once the cookies are cooled, arrange them in a single layer on 1 unlined baking sheet. Position an oven rack 6 inches (15 cm) below the broiler and preheat the broiler. Place a marshmallow half, cut side down, on the center of each cookie. Broil until the marshmallows are gooey and golden (watch carefully to prevent them from burning). Transfer the cookies to a wire rack and let cool. Just before serving, put a spoonful of cocoa powder in a fine-mesh sieve and lightly dust the cookies.

peppermint bark brownies

Chocolate and peppermint are a natural combination, especially around the holidays. These rich, tender brownies are spiked with peppermint extract, then topped with a thin, creamy layer of mint icing. Crushed candy canes take these treats over the top.

FOR THE CHOCOLATE-
MINT BROWNIES

4 oz (110 g) unsweetened
chocolate, chopped

½ cup (4 oz/115 g) unsalted
butter, plus more for greasing

1¼ cups (9 oz/250 g)
granulated sugar

1½ teaspoons
peppermint extract

¾ teaspoon vanilla extract

¼ teaspoon salt

3 large eggs

¾ cup (3 oz/90 g)
all-purpose flour

FOR THE
PEPPERMINT ICING

1 cup (4 oz/115 g)
confectioners' sugar

3 tablespoons
unsalted butter, at
cool room temperature

1 tablespoon whole milk,
plus more as needed

2 teaspoons
peppermint extract

½ cup crushed
peppermint canes
or candies (about
15–20 candies)

MAKES ABOUT 16 BROWNIES

Preheat the oven to 325°F (165°C). Grease an 8-inch (20-cm) square baking pan. Line the bottom and sides with parchment paper, letting the paper overhang on two opposite sides by 2 inches (5 cm).

To make the brownies, in a large saucepan over low heat, melt the butter and chocolate, stirring until smooth. Remove from the heat and let cool slightly, then whisk in the sugar, peppermint and vanilla extracts, and salt. Whisk in the eggs one at a time, whisking well after each addition. Continue to whisk until the mixture is velvety. Add the flour and whisk just until incorporated. Pour the batter into the prepared pan and spread evenly.

Bake until the top is just springy to the touch and a toothpick inserted into the center comes out with a few moist crumbs attached, about 40 minutes. Transfer the pan to a wire rack and let cool completely.

To make the icing, in a food processor, combine the confectioners' sugar, butter, milk, and peppermint extract and process until smooth, thinning the icing with more milk if necessary. The icing should be thick.

Use the parchment to lift the brownies from the pan and transfer to a work surface. Peel back the parchment from the sides. Spread the icing on top of the cooled brownies. Sprinkle the crushed candies over the top. Set aside for 30 minutes for the icing to set. Cut into squares and serve.

peppermint swirl macarons

French macarons, made from a gluten-free egg white and almond flour batter, are light and airy, crisp and chewy. This holiday version features red-and-white-swirled cookies with a rich white chocolate and peppermint filling. You can use this recipe to make nearly any flavor of macarons by just swapping out the frosting used to sandwich them together. The cookies will emerge very crisp from the oven, and they need a day in the refrigerator to soften, so be sure to plan in advance.

2 cups (8 oz/230 g) confectioners' sugar

1 cup (4 oz/130 g) superfine almond flour

3 large egg whites

1 teaspoon vanilla extract

¼ teaspoon cream of tartar

⅛ teaspoon salt

About 1 teaspoon red gel paste food coloring

½ recipe White Chocolate–Peppermint Frosting (page 172)

MAKES 24 COOKIES

Line 2 baking sheets with parchment paper. Using a 1½-inch (4-cm) circular guide (such as a biscuit cutter), draw 24 circles on each sheet of parchment, spacing them about 1 inch (2.5 cm) apart. Turn the parchment paper over. Combine 1 cup (4 oz/115 g) of the sugar and the almond flour in a sifter or fine-mesh sieve. Set aside.

In a large bowl, using an electric mixer on medium speed, beat the egg whites, vanilla, cream of tartar, and salt until foamy, about 2 minutes. Raise the speed to high and gradually beat in the remaining 1 cup (4 oz/115 g) sugar, beating to stiff peaks, 2–4 minutes. Sift about one-third of the sugar–almond flour mixture over the beaten whites. Using a rubber spatula, gently fold it in just until blended. Repeat to fold in the remaining sugar mixture in 2 more additions until incorporated. Continue to fold the mixture until the ingredients are completely combined and the batter flows in a slow, thick ribbon (about 40 strokes).

Fit a piping bag with a ⅜-inch (1-cm) round tip. Using a small, clean paintbrush, paint thin vertical stripes of the food coloring from tip to top against the side of the inside of the piping bag, spacing them evenly around the bag. Place the bag tip-end down in a glass and carefully spoon in the batter using a rubber spatula, trying not to disturb the lines of food coloring; leave about 2 inches (5 cm) free at the top. Gently twist the bag closed.

Holding the piping bag with the tip about ½ inch (12 mm) above the prepared baking sheet, pipe mounds of batter onto each sheet, using the circles as a template for each mound. Pipe even mounds spaced about 1 inch (2.5 cm) apart, making the mounds as smooth as possible by moving the bag off to one side after piping each mound. Tap each baking sheet firmly against the work surface 2 or 3 times to release any air bubbles. Let the cookies stand at room temperature until they look less wet and are a little tacky, 45–60 minutes.

Preheat the oven to 300°F (150°C). Bake 1 sheet at a time until the cookies have risen and set but not browned, about 20 minutes. The bottoms of the cookies should be dry and firm to the touch and not stick to the parchment paper; if they stick, bake them a few minutes longer. Transfer the sheet to a wire rack and let cool for 1 minute, then use a metal spatula to move the cookies directly to the rack. Repeat to bake the rest of the cookies. Let cool completely.

Spread about ½ teaspoon frosting over the flat side of half of the cookies. Top them with the remaining cookies, flat side down. Place the cookies in a single layer on a baking sheet, cover with plastic wrap, and refrigerate for at least 1 day or up to 3 days, or freeze for up to 6 months. (If frozen, thaw in the refrigerator before serving.) Serve chilled or at cool room temperature.

gingerbread cutout cookies

This spiced gingerbread cookie dough can be made into any shapes you like, from traditional gingerbread men to stars to snowflakes. Royal icing is quick to make and dries firm, so it's ideal for creating fun designs and decorations. Be sure to add any sugars, sprinkles, or candies to the icing while it's still wet so they will stay in place.

5 cups (21¼ oz/620 g) all-purpose flour

1 teaspoon baking soda

1 tablespoon ground ginger

1 teaspoon ground cinnamon

½ teaspoon ground cloves

½ teaspoon salt

1 cup (8 oz/225 g) unsalted butter, at cool room temperature

½ cup (3½ oz/100 g) firmly packed light brown sugar

½ cup (3½ oz/100 g) granulated sugar

1 large egg

1 cup (12 oz/340 g) light molasses

1 recipe Royal Icing (page 170)

Sparkle sugar, sprinkles, small candies, and/or mini chocolate chips, for decorating

MAKES 2–5 DOZEN COOKIES

In a bowl, whisk together the flour, baking soda, ginger, cinnamon, cloves, and salt. In a large bowl, using an electric mixer on high speed, beat the butter, brown sugar, and granulated sugar until fluffy and pale, about 2 minutes. Beat in the egg until well combined. Beat in the molasses until combined. Reduce the speed to low and beat in the flour mixture. Turn the dough out onto a floured work surface and divide into 4 equal portions. Shape each portion into a disk, wrap in plastic wrap, and refrigerate for at least 2 hours or up to 2 days.

Preheat the oven to 400°F (200°C). Line 2 baking sheets with parchment paper.

Working with 1 disk at a time, roll out the dough between 2 sheets of parchment paper to a thickness of about ¼ inch (6 mm). Using cookie cutters, cut out shapes. Use an offset spatula to transfer the shapes to a prepared baking sheet. Repeat with the remaining dough portions. Gather up the dough scraps, press them together, reroll, and cut out additional cookies. If the scraps of dough have become sticky, refrigerate them for 10 minutes before rerolling.

Bake the gingerbread cookies until lightly browned on the bottom, about 6 minutes. Transfer the baking sheets to wire racks and let cool for 5 minutes, then transfer the cookies to the racks and let cool completely.

Decorate with royal icing, sugars, and other decorations.

chocolate, raspberry & toasted almond bark

Chocolate bark is easy to make and can be personalized with any combination of dried fruit and nuts. This recipe makes good use of freeze-dried raspberries and almonds, but you can also try dried cherries and pistachios, freeze-dried strawberries and pecans, or dried blueberries and hazelnuts.

7 oz (200 g) bittersweet or semisweet chocolate, chopped

1 oz (30 g) unsweetened chocolate, chopped

¾ cup (3¾ oz/105 g) chopped whole almonds, toasted (page 74)

¾ cup freeze-dried raspberries

MAKES ABOUT ¾ LB (340 G) CANDY

Grease a rimmed baking sheet and line with parchment paper. Place the chocolates in a heatproof bowl set over but not touching barely simmering water in a saucepan and heat, stirring occasionally, until melted and smooth.

Stir ½ cup (2½ oz/70 g) of the almonds and ½ cup of the freeze-dried raspberries into the melted chocolate, then pour onto the prepared baking sheet, tilting to spread slightly. Sprinkle with the remaining ¼ cup each nuts and raspberries. Refrigerate uncovered until firm, about 1 hour.

Gently peel the chocolate bark from the parchment paper. Then, holding the candy with the parchment (to prevent fingerprints), break the chocolate into large irregular pieces. Serve.

chocolate-raspberry mini tarts

Thin chocolate pastry shells filled with clouds of raspberry cream and topped with fresh raspberries make these elegant mini tarts ideal for a gathering. Make the tart dough and line the pans well in advance, then bake and fill the pastry shells just before serving. Using a muffin pan is an easy way to form individual-size tartlets.

1 recipe Cocoa Tart Dough
(page 167)

1 cup (250 ml) heavy cream

2 tablespoons seedless
raspberry jam

12 fresh raspberries
for garnish

Confectioners' sugar,
for dusting

MAKES 12 TARTLETS

Lightly spray 12 standard muffin cups with cooking spray. On a lightly floured work surface, roll out the dough into a round about ⅛ inch (3 mm) thick. If the dough tears, press it back together. Using a 3¼-inch (8-cm) fluted cookie cutter, cut out as many rounds as possible. Gather up the scraps, press them together, roll out, and cut out more rounds as needed to total 12 rounds. Transfer each round to a prepared muffin cup, gently pressing it evenly into the bottom and partly up the sides. Place the lined muffin cups in the freezer to firm up for 30 minutes before baking.

Preheat the oven to 350°F (180°C). Bake the tartlet shells until cooked through, about 15 minutes. Transfer the pan to a wire rack and let the tartlet shells cool in the muffin cups for 10 minutes, then carefully remove the tartlet shells from the muffin cups and let cool completely on the rack.

When the shells are cool, make the filling. In a bowl, using an electric mixer on medium-high speed, beat together the cream and raspberry jam until stiff peaks form, about 5 minutes. The peaks should stand straight when the beaters are lifted; be careful not to overwhip.

Spoon the filling into a pastry bag fitted with a large star tip. Pipe the cream into the tartlet shells, dividing it evenly. Top each tartlet with a raspberry. Using a fine-mesh sieve, dust the tops with confectioners' sugar. Serve right away.

s'mores fudge

The addition of evaporated milk to this silky fudge eliminates the need for precise cooking temperatures and guarantees a creamy consistency. You could stop there, but turn these into next-level fudge with the addition of mini marshmallows and crunched-up graham crackers. Wrap pieces of the fudge in parchment paper–lined boxes to give to family and friends.

1½ cups (10½ oz/300 g) sugar

½ cup (4 oz/115 g) evaporated milk

2 tablespoons unsalted butter, plus more for greasing

¼ teaspoon salt

2 cups (12 oz/340 g) semisweet or bittersweet chocolate chips

2 teaspoons vanilla extract

1 cup (1¾ oz/50 g) mini marshmallows

1 cup (3½ oz/100 g) roughly broken graham crackers (about 8 crackers)

MAKES ABOUT 36 SQUARES

Grease a 9-inch (23-cm) square baking pan.

In a large saucepan over medium heat, bring the butter, sugar, evaporated milk, and salt to a boil, stirring constantly. Reduce the heat to medium-low and simmer, stirring constantly, for 5 minutes. Remove from the heat and stir in the chocolate chips. Continue to stir gently until the chocolate melts and the mixture is completely smooth. Stir in the vanilla. Gently fold in the marshmallows and graham crackers.

Pour the mixture into the prepared pan and spread evenly. Cover with plastic wrap and refrigerate until firm, about 3 hours. Cut into squares and serve.

chocolate-hazelnut pastry wreath

With only a few sheets of purchased puff pastry and a jar of chocolate-hazelnut spread, you can create a showstopping dessert. Here, puff pastry sheets are layered with a thin filling, then cut and twisted into a spectacular wreath. Frozen puff pastry is sold in sheets ranging from 9 to 11 inches (23 to 28 cm). Either size will work fine; just adjust the amount of filling.

1 lb (450 g) frozen puff pastry, thawed

½ cup chocolate-hazelnut spread, such as Nutella

1 large egg, lightly beaten with 1 teaspoon water

Confectioners' sugar, for dusting

MAKES 8 SERVINGS

Preheat the oven to 400°F (200°C). Line a baking sheet with parchment paper.

Place 1 sheet of puff pastry on a lightly floured work surface. Using a rolling pin, roll out the pastry into a 10- or 12-inch (25- or 30-cm) square. Using a 10- or 12-inch (25- or 30-cm) plate or bowl as a guide, cut around the circumference with a knife to make a round. Slide the pastry round onto the prepared baking sheet. Repeat to roll out and cut the second sheet of puff pastry. Place the second round on a sheet of parchment paper, then place it on top of the first round. Refrigerate the rounds for 15 minutes.

Remove 1 round of puff pastry from the refrigerator. Gently spread the chocolate-hazelnut spread on the round, leaving a 1-inch (2.5-cm) border around the edge. Lightly brush the uncovered edge with some of the egg wash. Carefully place the second round of pastry over the first, lining up the edges and gently pressing them together. Lightly brush the top with some of the egg wash.

Place a drinking glass upside down in the middle. Use a sharp paring knife or pizza cutter to cut the pastry in strips from the glass to the edge to create "rays." Start by cutting the pastry into equal quarters, then cut each quarter in half, then each half in half again to form 16 rays. Remove the glass and gently twist each ray a few times. Lightly brush the pastry with more egg wash.

Bake until the pastry is golden brown and cooked through, about 30 minutes. Remove the baking sheet from the oven and slide the tart onto a wire rack. Let cool. Dust the tart with confectioners' sugar and serve.

raspberry linzer heart cookies

Linzer cookies are a variation of the Austrian linzertorte, a nut-and-jam tart with a shortbread-like crust. You can use any nuts you like—almonds, walnuts, pecans—but the most traditional are hazelnuts. This recipe uses raspberry jam, but apricot or even red currant would also be delicious. Cut these into heart shapes for Valentine's Day, or into rounds for any other time of the year.

2 cups (8 oz/330 g) almonds, walnuts, or pecans, toasted (page 74)

2½ cups (11 oz/310 g) all-purpose flour, plus more for dusting

1 cup (8 oz/225 g) unsalted butter, at cool room temperature

1 cup (4 oz/115 g) confectioners' sugar, plus more for dusting

2 large egg yolks

½ cup (2 oz/60 g) cornstarch

Raspberry jam

MAKES ABOUT 4 DOZEN COOKIES

In a food processor, combine the nuts and 1 cup (4¼ oz/115 g) of the flour and process until the nuts are finely ground. Set aside.

In a bowl, using an electric mixer on medium speed, beat together the butter and confectioners' sugar until fluffy, about 4 minutes. Beat in the egg yolks one at a time, beating well after each addition. Reduce the speed to low and beat in the nut mixture, the remaining 1½ cups (6½ oz/180 g) flour, and the cornstarch until blended. Turn the dough out, divide into 4 equal portions, and shape each portion into a disk. Wrap each disk in plastic wrap and refrigerate overnight.

Place a rack in the upper third of the oven and preheat to 325°F (165°C). Line 2 baking sheets with parchment paper.

On a lightly floured work surface, roll out a dough disk ¼ inch (6 mm) thick. Using a 2½-inch (6-mm) heart-shaped cookie cutter, cut out the cookies. Transfer half of the cookies to a prepared baking sheet. Using a 1½-inch (4-mm) heart-shaped cookie cutter, cut a heart in the center of each of the remaining cookies, creating heart frames to use as cookie tops. Transfer to the other prepared baking sheet. Gather up the dough scraps and smaller hearts, press them together, and cut out more cookie tops and bottoms. Repeat with the remaining disks.

Bake one sheet at a time, just until golden, about 15 minutes for the bottoms and 12 minutes for the tops. Transfer the baking sheets to wire racks and let cool completely on the racks.

Using a small butter knife, spread raspberry on the solid heart-shaped cookies. Using a fine-mesh sieve, dust the heart frames evenly with confectioners' sugar. Place the sugar-dusted frames atop the larger hearts, and serve.

chestnut torte with mocha buttercream

Warm roasted chestnuts are a common sight on European street corners in the winter. Chestnut purée is available at most upscale or international markets, and it adds delicate flavor to this light gluten-free torte that is topped with luscious rum-spiked mocha buttercream frosting.

1½ cups (6 oz/210 g) almonds, toasted (page 74)

6 large eggs, separated

1½ cups (10½ oz/300 g) sugar

1 tablespoon vanilla extract

2 cups (1 lb/450 g) chestnut purée, pushed through a sieve

1 recipe Mocha Buttercream (page 175)

MAKES 10 SERVINGS

Preheat the oven to 350°F (180°C). Grease two 8-inch (20-cm) springform pans. Dust with flour, then tap out any excess. In a food processor, process the almonds until they are very finely ground. Set aside.

Place the egg yolks and 1 cup (7 oz/200 g) of the sugar in a heatproof bowl. Set the bowl over but not touching barely simmering water in a saucepan. Using an electric mixer on medium speed, beat for a few minutes until warm. Remove the bowl from the pan and beat on high speed until the mixture is very thick and pale, about 8 minutes. Beat in the vanilla, then the chestnut purée and ground almonds.

In another bowl, using clean beaters, beat the egg whites on medium speed until soft peaks form, about 3 minutes. Gradually beat in the remaining ½ cup (3½ oz/100 g) sugar until the mixture is stiff but not dry. Stir one-third of the whites into the chestnut mixture, then fold in the remaining whites. Divide the batter between the prepared pans.

Bake until the cakes are pale gold and pull away from the sides of the pans, 40–50 minutes. Transfer the pans to wire racks and let cool, then remove the pan sides.

Place 1 cake on a serving plate and frost it, then place the second cake on top. Frost the top and sides. Refrigerate until the frosting is set, about 30 minutes, then bring to room temperature before serving.

sweet potato pie with pecan streusel

Sweet potato custard pie is a great alternative to pumpkin pie, whether on your holiday table or as a sweet end to a Sunday supper. This one has a crunchy toasted-pecan streusel surprise on top, but you can leave it off to keep it simple. Make sure you bake the pie only until the filling is set but still has a slight wobble.

1 recipe Flaky Pie Dough, Single Crust (page 166)

FOR THE FILLING

2 cups peeled, cooked, and mashed sweet potatoes (page 115; from about 2½ lb/1.1 kg potatoes)

1 cup (7½ oz/210 g) firmly packed light brown sugar

1 can (12-fl-oz) evaporated milk

3 large eggs

¼ cup (2 oz/60 g) unsalted butter, melted

1 tablespoon vanilla extract

1 teaspoon ground cinnamon

¼ teaspoon ground nutmeg

¼ teaspoon salt

1 recipe Pecan Streusel (page 118)

1 recipe Whipped Cream (page 176), for serving

MAKES 8 SERVINGS

Prepare the dough and chill as directed. On a lightly floured work surface, roll out the dough into a round at least 12 inches (30 cm) in diameter and about ⅛ inch (3 mm) thick. Transfer to a 9-inch (23-cm) pie pan and ease into the pan. Trim the overhang to 1 inch (2.5 cm), fold the edge of the dough under itself to create a rim, and crimp the edges to seal. Pierce the bottom of the crust all over with a fork and freeze for 30 minutes.

Preheat the oven to 400°F (200°C). Line the pie shell with aluminum foil and fill with pie weights. Bake until the dough starts to look dry, about 15 minutes. Remove the foil and weights and continue to bake until the crust is just barely golden, about 5 minutes longer. Transfer to a wire rack and let cool completely. Reduce the oven temperature to 350°F (180°C).

To make the filling, in a food processor, blend the sweet potatoes until smooth. Add the brown sugar, evaporated milk, eggs, butter, vanilla, cinnamon, nutmeg, and salt, and blend until smooth, stopping occasionally to scrape down the sides. Pour the filling into the crust.

Bake for 30 minutes. Remove the pie from the oven and gently sprinkle the pecan streusel over the top in an even layer. Continue to bake until the center is set and the topping is golden brown, 15–20 minutes longer, covering the edges with aluminum foil if they brown too quickly. Transfer the pan to a wire rack and let cool completely. Serve at room temperature or chilled, topped with whipped cream.

pear-almond custard tart

This delicately flavored tart, filled with vanilla-poached pears, brandy-spiked custard, and sugary toasted almonds, is a memorable dessert suitable for any holiday gathering. To turn this into an apple tart, gently sauté three peeled, cored, and sliced apples in 1 tablespoon butter until they just start to become tender. Spread the apples evenly in the partially baked crust, pour over the custard, and proceed with the recipe from there.

1 recipe Flaky Pie Dough, Single Crust (page 166)

FOR THE
POACHED PEARS

¾ cup (5 oz/140 g) sugar

3 ripe but firm pears, preferably Bosc, peeled, quartered, and cored

Peel of 1 orange, removed in strips with a vegetable peeler

½ vanilla bean

FOR THE CUSTARD

1 large egg

¼ cup (1¾ oz/50 g) sugar, plus 1 tablespoon

3 tablespoons all-purpose flour, plus more for dusting

½ cup (125 ml) heavy cream

2 tablespoons brandy or 1 teaspoon vanilla extract

Pinch of salt

¼ cup (¾ oz/25 g) sliced almonds, lightly toasted (page 74)

MAKES ONE 10-INCH
(25-CM) TART

Prepare the dough and chill as directed.

To poach the pears, cut a circle of parchment paper that will fit in a medium saucepan. Cut a 1-inch (2.5-cm) circle in the middle of the parchment. Set aside.

In the saucepan over high heat, bring 3 cups (720 ml) water and the sugar to a boil. Reduce the heat to medium and add the pears and orange peel. Split the vanilla bean and scrape out the seeds with the back of a paring knife; add the pod and seeds to the saucepan. Lay the parchment in the saucepan to submerge the pears. Adjust the heat so that the liquid simmers gently. Poach the pears until just tender, about 15 minutes. Remove from the heat and let cool in the poaching liquid.

On a lightly floured work surface, roll out the dough into a 13-inch (33-cm) round about ⅛ inch (3 mm) thick. Transfer to a 10-inch (25-cm) tart pan with a removable bottom and ease into the pan, patting it firmly into the bottom and up the sides of the pan. Trim off any excess dough by running a rolling pin across the top of the pan. Press the dough into the sides to extend it slightly above the rim. Prick the bottom of the crust all over with a fork and freeze for 30 minutes.

Preheat the oven to 400°F (200°C). Line the tart shell with aluminum foil and fill with pie weights or dried beans. Bake until the dough starts to look dry, about 15 minutes. Remove the foil and weights and continue to bake until the crust is lightly golden, about 5 minutes longer. Transfer to a wire rack and let cool completely. Reduce the oven temperature to 350°F (180°C).

Cut each pear quarter lengthwise into 4 slices, then lay most of the pear slices in the crust in an overlapping circle close to the rim. Use the remaining slices to fill the middle.

To make the custard, in a bowl, using an electric mixer on medium speed, beat together the egg and the ¼ cup (1¾ oz/50 g) sugar until thick and pale. Beat in the flour and then the cream, brandy, and salt. Pour the custard evenly over the pears. Bake until the custard starts to puff up, about 10 minutes. Sprinkle the toasted almonds and the 1 tablespoon sugar over the top of the tart. Continue to bake until the custard is set and lightly browned, 15–20 minutes longer. Remove the pan from the oven and let cool on a wire rack until warm or at room temperature before slicing and serving.

bittersweet chocolate & salted caramel tart

Layers of chocolate and creamy caramel fill a chocolate crust in this exquisite tart.
A sprinkle of sea salt over the top intensifies the flavors and adds sparkle and crunch.
Thin wedges of this dessert would be the perfect ending to an elegant meal.

1 recipe Cocoa Tart Dough
(page 167)

FOR THE
CARAMEL FILLING

1 cup (7 oz/200 g) sugar

⅔ cup (160 ml) heavy cream

3 tablespoons unsalted butter

¼ teaspoon salt

FOR THE
GANACHE FILLING

6 oz (170 g) bittersweet
chocolate, chopped

¾ cup (180 ml) heavy cream

Flake sea salt, such as Maldon

MAKES 8 SERVINGS

Prepare the dough and chill as directed. On a lightly floured work surface, roll out the dough into a round about ⅛ inch (3 mm) thick. If the dough tears, press it back together. Carefully transfer to a 9½-inch (24-cm) tart pan with a removable bottom and ease into the pan, patting it firmly into the bottom and up the sides of the pan. Trim off any excess dough by running a rolling pin across the top of the pan. Press the dough into the sides to extend it slightly above the rim. Prick the bottom of the tart shell all over with a fork. Refrigerate or freeze until firm, about 30 minutes.

To make the caramel filling, in a saucepan over medium-high heat, combine the sugar and 3 tablespoons water, cover, and bring to a simmer. Once the sugar starts to melt, uncover and swirl the pan until the sugar dissolves, about 3 minutes. Continue to simmer, uncovered and swirling the pan occasionally, until the sugar turns a deep amber-brown, 2–4 minutes. Remove from the heat, carefully add the cream (the caramel will splatter), and whisk until smooth. Whisk in the butter and salt and let cool to room temperature.

Preheat the oven to 375°F (190°C). Place the tart shell on a baking sheet. Line the tart shell with aluminum foil and fill with pie weights or dried beans. Bake until the dough starts to look dry, about 10 minutes. Remove the foil and weights and continue to bake until the crust is set, about 7 minutes longer. Transfer to a wire rack and let cool completely. Spread the caramel into the cooled tart shell. Refrigerate until set, about 1 hour.

To make the ganache filling, place the chocolate in a heatproof bowl. In a saucepan over medium-low heat, bring the cream to a simmer and pour over the chocolate. Let stand for about 5 minutes, then whisk until smooth. Pour the chocolate mixture over the caramel, smoothing the top. Refrigerate until firm, at least 2 hours or up to 2 days, covering the tart with plastic wrap once the chocolate is set.

To serve, let the tart stand at room temperature for about 15 minutes to soften slightly. Sprinkle with a little sea salt, and serve.

spiced apple strudel

Traditional strudel pastry is difficult to make from scratch, but thin layers of filo dough make a great substitute in this classic Austrian and Central European dessert. Filo dough can be found in the freezer section of the grocery store. Be sure to keep the dough sheets under a barely damp kitchen towel to keep them moist while you work.

12 sheets filo dough, thawed if frozen

½ cup (4 oz/115 g) unsalted butter, melted and cooled

7 teaspoons granulated sugar

1 lb (450 g) tart-crisp baking apples, such as Honeycrisp, Pink Lady, or Gala, peeled, cored, and diced (about 3 cups)

1 cup (7 oz) mixed chopped dried fruit such as sour cherries, apricots, cranberries, and/or currants

½ cup (3½ oz/100 g) firmly packed light brown sugar

¼ teaspoon ground cinnamon

⅛ teaspoon freshly grated nutmeg

MAKES 6–8 SERVINGS

Place a rack in the lower third of the oven and preheat to 375°F (190°C). Line a baking sheet with parchment paper.

Working with 1 filo sheet at a time and keeping the others covered with a barely damp kitchen towel to prevent them from drying out, place the first sheet on the prepared baking sheet. Using a pastry brush, brush well with some of the melted butter. Lay a second filo on top of the first and brush again with butter. Sprinkle with 1 teaspoon of the granulated sugar. Repeat, brushing every sheet with butter and sprinkling every other sheet with 1 teaspoon granulated sugar, until all the filo is used.

In a large bowl, toss together the apples, dried fruit, brown sugar, cinnamon, and nutmeg. Arrange the apple filling along one long side of the filo, positioning it about 1 inch (2.5 cm) from the edge. Fold the edge of the filo over the filling, then carefully roll up the filo into a log with the seam side down. Brush the log with melted butter and sprinkle with the remaining 1 teaspoon granulated sugar.

Bake until the filo is golden and the apples are tender when pierced with a knife, 45–55 minutes. Transfer the pan to a wire rack and let cool for 30 minutes. To serve, transfer to a long platter and cut crosswise into pieces.

blood orange tartlets

Blood oranges are in season for a short time during winter, and they lend a stunning ruby-rose color to the curd that fills these tartlets. If you cannot find them, you can use regular fresh orange juice, but because blood orange juice is slightly tarter than other varieties, reduce the amount of sugar in the filling to ⅔ cup (4¾ oz/140 g).

1 recipe Cream Cheese Tartlet Dough (page 168)

2 large eggs, plus 3 large egg yolks

¾ cup (5 oz/140 g) sugar

½ cup (125 ml) fresh blood orange juice, strained

2 tablespoons fresh lemon juice, strained

2 teaspoons finely grated blood orange zest, plus more for garnish (optional)

½ cup (4 oz/115 g) unsalted butter, cut into pieces

1 recipe Whipped Cream (page 176)

MAKES 6 TARTLETS

Prepare the dough and chill as directed. Cut the dough into 6 equal portions, and place one portion in each of six 4-inch (10-cm) tartlet pans. Press the dough evenly into the bottom and up the sides of each pan until it is even with the rim. Trim the dough if there's any overhang. Freeze until the dough is firm, about 30 minutes.

Preheat the oven to 400°F (200°C). Line the tartlet shells with foil and fill with pie weights or dried beans. Place on a baking sheet and bake until the dough starts to look dry, about 15 minutes. Remove the weights and foil and continue to bake until the crusts are lightly browned, about 5 minutes longer. Let cool on the baking sheet. Reduce the oven temperature to 325°F (165°C).

In a heatproof bowl, whisk together the eggs, egg yolks, sugar, orange juice, lemon juice, and orange zest. Set the bowl over but not touching barely simmering water in a saucepan and whisk constantly until the mixture is thick enough to coat the back of a spoon and registers 160°F (71°C) on an instant-read thermometer, about 12 minutes. Remove the bowl from the heat and pour the mixture through a medium-mesh sieve into a bowl. Add the butter and stir until the butter melts and is incorporated. Let stand for 10 minutes, then spoon the filling into the cooled tartlet shells.

Bake until the centers are set, 12–15 minutes. Transfer the baking sheet to a wire rack and let cool for 20 minutes. Cover and refrigerate for at least 3 hours or up to overnight. The filling will thicken further. To serve, unmold each tartlet and top with a dollop of whipped cream and a sprinkle of zest, if you like.

mini lemon poppy seed drizzle cakes

These lemony cupcakes are like a burst of sunshine on a winter's day. Plenty of fresh lemon zest adds zing, but if you want an extra burst of lemon, add ½ teaspoon lemon extract to the batter. A simple lemon glaze adorns these cakes, made even more celebratory with sparkling sugar or sprinkles, a pinch of poppy seeds on top, or even a few slices of candied lemon peel.

FOR THE LEMON POPPY SEED CAKES

2¼ cups (10 oz/270 g) all-purpose flour

2 tablespoons poppy seeds

1½ teaspoons baking powder

½ teaspoon salt

¾ cup (6 oz/170 g) unsalted butter, at cool room temperature

1½ cups (10½ oz/300 g) granulated sugar

2 teaspoons finely grated lemon zest

2 large eggs

¾ cup (180 ml) whole milk

FOR THE LEMON GLAZE

2 cups (8 oz/230 g) confectioners' sugar, sifted

3 tablespoons fresh lemon juice

MAKES 24 MINI CAKES

Preheat the oven to 325°F (165°C). Line 24 standard muffin cups with paper liners.

To make the cakes, in a bowl, whisk together the flour, poppy seeds, baking powder, and salt. In a large bowl, using an electric mixer on medium-high speed, beat the butter, granulated sugar, and lemon zest until fluffy and pale, about 3 minutes. Add the eggs one at a time, beating well after adding each one. Stop the mixer and scrape down the sides of the bowl. Reduce the speed to low, add half of the flour mixture, then the milk, and then the remaining flour mixture, beating until combined.

Divide the batter evenly among the muffin cups, filling each three-fourths full. Bake until golden brown and a toothpick inserted into the center of a cupcake comes out clean, 18–20 minutes. Let the cakes cool in the pan for 10 minutes, then transfer them to wire racks to cool completely.

To make the glaze, in a bowl, whisk together the confectioners' sugar and lemon juice. Spoon some glaze on top of each cooled cake and use the back of the spoon to spread it to the edge. Let the glaze dry for about 20 minutes, then serve.

chocolate espresso heart cake

With only a round cake pan and a square cake pan, you can create this espresso-infused chocolate cake in the shape of a heart—perfect for a Valentine's dinner. A thick layer of rich chocolate frosting and plenty of edible flowers provide the finishing touch. Or, decorate the top with fresh raspberries and a dusting of confectioners' sugar.

FOR THE CHOCOLATE
ESPRESSO CAKE

2½ cups (11 oz/310 g)
all-purpose flour

1 cup (3 oz/90 g)
unsweetened cocoa powder

2 teaspoons baking powder

½ teaspoon baking soda

½ teaspoon salt

2 cups (14 oz/400 g) sugar

3 large eggs

1½ cups (375 ml) buttermilk

½ cup (125 ml) avocado or
canola oil

1 tablespoon vanilla extract

6 oz (170 g) bittersweet
chocolate, melted and cooled

4 teaspoons espresso powder

1 recipe Chocolate Frosting
(page 172)

Edible flowers, for decorating

MAKES 8 SERVINGS

Preheat the oven to 350°F (180°C). Grease an 8-inch (20-cm) round cake pan and an 8-inch (20-cm) square cake pan, line the bottoms of the pans with parchment paper, then grease the parchment. Dust with flour, then tap out any excess.

To make the cake, in a bowl, sift together the flour, cocoa powder, baking powder, baking soda, and salt. Set aside.

In a bowl, using an electric mixer on medium speed, beat together the sugar, eggs, buttermilk, oil, and vanilla until blended, about 2 minutes. Reduce the speed to low, slowly add the flour mixture, and beat until incorporated, stopping the mixer to scrape down the sides of the bowl as needed. Add the melted chocolate and espresso powder and beat until combined. Raise the speed to high and beat for 30 seconds.

Divide the batter evenly between the prepared pans and spread evenly. Bake until a toothpick inserted into the center of the cakes comes out clean, 30–35 minutes. Transfer the pans to wire racks and let cool for 10 minutes, then invert the cakes onto the racks and let cool completely.

To assemble, cut the round cake in half crosswise. Orient the square cake as a diamond. Frost the cut sides of the half rounds with chocolate frosting and place them against the top sides of the diamond to form a heart shape, pressing gently to adhere. Spread the remaining frosting over the entire surface of the cake. Decorate with edible flowers and serve.

mocha bûche de noël

Often served at Christmastime, this traditional roulade cake is decorated to look like a yule log. This version uses cocoa and espresso in the cake itself, which is then filled with mocha buttercream before being rolled. Dark chocolate ganache covers the exterior of the cake, decorated to look like the bark on a log. If you like, decorate the log with meringue or marzipan "mushrooms" or berries.

6 large eggs

¾ cup (5 oz/140 g) granulated sugar

1 teaspoon espresso powder

¾ cup (3 oz/90 g) all-purpose flour

2 tablespoons unsweetened cocoa powder

¼ teaspoon salt

2 tablespoons unsalted butter, melted, plus more for greasing

Confectioners' sugar

1 recipe Mocha Buttercream (page 175)

1 recipe Chocolate Ganache (page 169)

MAKES 12 SERVINGS

Preheat the oven to 350°F (180°C). Grease a 10-by-15-inch (25-by-38-cm) jelly roll pan, line the bottom with parchment paper, then grease the parchment. Dust with flour, then tap out any excess.

In a large heatproof bowl, combine the eggs, granulated sugar, and espresso powder. Set the bowl over but not touching barely simmering water in a saucepan and whisk just until warm to the touch. Remove from the heat. Using an electric mixer on high speed, beat the mixture until tripled in volume and soft peaks form, about 3 minutes. In a sifter, combine the flour, cocoa powder, and salt. Sift directly onto the egg mixture. Using a rubber spatula, gently fold the mixtures together. Drizzle the butter over the mixture, then fold it in.

Pour the batter into the prepared pan, spreading it into an even layer. Bake until a toothpick inserted into the center of the cake comes out clean, about 15 minutes. Transfer the pan to a wire rack and let cool completely.

Place a large sheet of parchment paper on a work surface. Using a sifter or sieve, generously dust the paper with confectioners' sugar. Invert the jelly roll pan onto the paper and lift off the pan. Carefully peel off the parchment paper from the bottom of the cake.

Spread the buttercream evenly over the cake. Beginning at a long side, roll up the cake jelly roll style. Using a sharp knife, cut off the ends on the diagonal so that each piece is 1 inch (2.5 cm) long on one side and 3 inches (7.5 cm) long on the other. Place one piece, cut side to cake, on top of the cake toward one end. Place the other piece, cut side to cake, on the side of the cake toward the other end. The cake should resemble a log with cut limbs.

Stir the ganache until spreadable, then frost the cake, including all the ends. Using a fork, run the tines in circles on the ends and cut limbs of the log. Then run the tines the length of the log to simulate bark. Just before serving, sift confectioners' sugar over the log to simulate snow. Slice crosswise to serve.

steamed figgy pudding

Quintessentially British, steamed puddings made with a mixture of dried fruits, candied peel, and spices, are often prepared months in advance. They are sometimes steeped in spirits and set alight when serving. This version is more approachable, similar to a rich bread pudding with chewy dried fruit. Serve drizzled with brandy or bourbon.

1½ cups (7½ oz/210 g) dried figs, tough stem ends trimmed

½ cup (3 oz/85 g) dried currants

8 slices good-quality white sandwich bread, crusts removed, torn into pea-sized crumbs

1¼ cups (5½ oz/155 g) all-purpose flour

7 tablespoons (3½ oz/105 g) unsalted butter, at cool room temperature, plus more for greasing

½ cup (3½ oz/100 g) firmly packed dark brown sugar

3 large eggs

1 cup (250 ml) whole milk

1 teaspoon vanilla extract

2 tablespoons chopped candied orange peel

1 tablespoon finely grated orange zest

1 recipe Whipped Cream (page 176), for serving

MAKES 8–10 SERVINGS

Preheat the oven to 300°F (150°C). Grease a 1½-qt (1.4-L) pudding mold. In a small saucepan over medium-high heat, bring the figs, currants, and 2 cups (480 ml) water to a boil. Reduce the heat to low and simmer, uncovered, until the figs are tender but still hold their shape, about 20 minutes. Remove from the heat and let stand in the cooking liquid.

Using a slotted spoon, transfer the figs and currants to a bowl; reserve the cooking liquid. Halve 8–10 of the figs lengthwise and press them, cut side down, in a decorative pattern in the prepared mold. Finely chop the remaining figs.

In a bowl, stir together the bread crumbs and flour. In another bowl, using an electric mixer on medium-high speed, beat the butter and brown sugar until fluffy, about 3–4 minutes. Add the eggs one at a time, beating well after each addition. Beat in the milk and vanilla. Stir in the candied orange peel, orange zest, and currants and chopped figs. Stir in half of the flour mixture, then stir in the remaining flour mixture. Pour the batter into the mold and fasten the lid.

Place the mold on a rack in a large pot with a lid and pour in boiling water to reach halfway up the sides of the mold. Bring to a boil over high heat, reduce the heat to medium-low, cover the pot, and boil for 2 hours, being careful not to let the water boil over. Replenish the water as needed to maintain the level.

Remove the mold from the water using oven mitts and let stand for 15 minutes. Remove the lid, invert the mold onto a platter, and tap gently to release the pudding.

In a small pan over high heat, bring the reserved fig liquid to a boil and cook until reduced to ½ cup (120 ml) syrup, about 5 minutes.

Serve wedges drizzled with syrup and topped with whipped cream.

sticky toffee pudding

Called "pudding" because of its British origins, these tender date-studded cakes are doused in a "sticky" toffee sauce made from dark brown sugar, butter, and cream. They make a festive ending to a holiday party or other special occasion. Serve with lightly whipped cream or a scoop of vanilla ice cream if you like.

FOR THE DATE CAKES

½ cup (2½ oz/70 g) pitted and finely chopped dates

¾ teaspoon baking soda

¾ cup (180 ml) boiling water

¼ cup (2 oz/60 g) unsalted butter, at cool room temperature, plus more for greasing

¾ cup (5½ oz/155 g) firmly packed dark brown sugar

2 large eggs

2 teaspoons vanilla extract

1 cup (4¼ oz/120 g) all-purpose flour

1¼ teaspoons baking powder

½ teaspoon salt

FOR THE TOFFEE SAUCE

¼ cup (2 oz/60 g) unsalted butter

¾ cup (5½ oz/155 g) firmly packed dark brown sugar

¾ cup (180 ml) heavy cream

2 teaspoons vanilla extract

Pinch of salt

MAKES 8 PUDDINGS

Preheat the oven to 350°F (180°C). Grease eight ½-cup (4-fl-oz) custard cups or individual baking pans. Dust with flour, then tap out any excess. Place the cups on a baking sheet.

To make the date cakes, in a small bowl, combine the dates and baking soda with the boiling water. Let stand until cool, about 10 minutes. In a bowl, using an electric mixer on medium speed, beat the butter and sugar until light and fluffy, about 5 minutes. Add the eggs one at a time, beating well after each addition. Beat in the vanilla. Add the flour, baking powder, and salt, and stir to combine. Add the date mixture and stir well. The batter will be thin. Divide the batter among the prepared custard cups, filling them about two-thirds full.

Bake until the puddings are puffed and a toothpick inserted into the center comes out clean, about 20 minutes.

Meanwhile, make the toffee sauce: In a saucepan over medium heat, melt the butter. Add the brown sugar and cream and whisk until the sauce gets sticky, about 5 minutes. Stir in the vanilla and salt.

To serve, unmold each warm pudding onto a plate and drizzle the toffee sauce over the top.

chocolate florentines

Elegant almond Florentines are lacy, thin, crisp cookies drizzled with chocolate glaze. Work quickly after removing the batter from the heat because it stiffens as it cools; a small cookie scoop helps portion the batter quickly. For an extra treat, serve these with a scoop of gelato.

FOR THE COOKIES

¼ cup (1 oz/30 g) all-purpose flour

1 teaspoon grated orange zest

½ cup (3½ oz/100 g) sugar

5 tablespoons (2½ oz/75 g) unsalted butter, cut into pieces

¼ cup (60 ml) heavy cream

2 tablespoons (1½ oz/40 g) honey

¾ cup (2¼ oz/90 g) sliced blanched almonds

FOR THE CHOCOLATE GLAZE

6 oz (170 g) semisweet chocolate, finely chopped

½ cup (4 oz/115 g) unsalted butter

1 tablespoon light corn syrup

MAKES ABOUT 2 DOZEN COOKIES

Preheat the oven to 325°F (165°C). Line 2 baking sheets with parchment paper.

To make the cookies, in a small bowl, stir together the flour and orange zest until the zest is coated. Set aside.

In a saucepan over low heat, combine the sugar, butter, cream, and honey. Cook, stirring, until the butter melts and the sugar dissolves. Raise the heat to medium-high and bring to a boil, stirring constantly, then boil for 2 minutes. Remove from the heat and stir in the almonds, followed by the flour mixture. The batter will be thick. Drop the batter by 2-teaspoon scoops onto the prepared baking sheets, spacing the cookies about 3 inches (7.5 cm) apart. Flatten each cookie with the back of the spoon.

Bake the cookies, 1 sheet at a time, until they spread to about 3 inches (7.5 cm), are bubbling vigorously, and have light brown edges, 8–10 minutes. Transfer the baking sheets to wire racks and let the cookies cool for 10 minutes. Using a wide spatula, transfer the cookies to the racks and let cool completely.

To make the chocolate glaze, place the chocolate, butter, and corn syrup in a large heatproof bowl set over but not touching barely simmering water in a saucepan and heat, stirring often, until the chocolate and butter are melted, about 4 minutes. Remove from the heat and pour the glaze through a fine-mesh sieve into a bowl. Let cool to 92°F (33°C) before using.

Using a spoon, drizzle the chocolate glaze over the top of each cookie. Let stand until the glaze sets, about 30 minutes.

VARIATION *To make a vanilla glaze, sift 1 cup (4 oz/125 g) confectioners' sugar into a small bowl. Add 3 tablespoons heavy cream and ½ teaspoon vanilla and stir until smooth, about 1 minute. Drizzle the vanilla glaze over the top of each cookie.*

spiced apple honey cake

Applesauce adds sweetness and moisture to this spice cake, which can be dressed up with whipped honey frosting and decorated with rosemary "trees" and gingerbread cookies cut into the shapes of animals. For a brunch-worthy version of the cake, cut the cake recipe in half, omit the frosting, and dust with confectioners' sugar, then serve with sautéed apples.

2 cups (9 oz/240 g) cake flour

1½ teaspoons baking soda

1 teaspoon baking powder

¾ teaspoon ground cinnamon

¾ teaspoon ground cardamom

¼ teaspoon salt

¾ cup (6 oz/170 g) unsalted butter, at cool room temperature, plus more for greasing

1¼ cups (9½ oz/270 g) firmly packed light brown sugar

3 large eggs

1 teaspoon vanilla extract

1 cup (225 g) unsweetened applesauce, at room temperature

⅔ cup (160 ml) whole milk, at room temperature

1 recipe Whipped Honey Frosting (page 173)

MAKES 10–12 SERVINGS

Preheat the oven to 350°F (180°C). Grease two 8-inch (20-cm) round cake pans, line the bottoms of the pans with parchment paper, then grease the parchment. Dust with flour, then tap out any excess.

In a medium bowl, whisk together the flour, baking soda, baking powder, cinnamon, cardamom, and salt. In a large bowl, using an electric mixer on medium-high speed, beat the butter and brown sugar until light and fluffy, 2–3 minutes. Add the eggs one at a time, beating well after each addition. Beat in the vanilla. Turn off the mixer and scrape down the sides of the bowl.

In a liquid measuring cup, combine the applesauce and milk. Add about one-third of the flour mixture to the mixing bowl. Mix on low speed just until blended. Pour in about half of the applesauce mixture and mix just until combined. Add about half of the remaining flour mixture and mix just until blended. Pour in the remaining applesauce mixture and mix just until combined. Add the remaining flour mixture and mix just until blended. Turn off the mixer, scrape down the sides of the bowl, and give the batter a final stir with a spatula.

Divide the batter evenly between the prepared cake pans and spread in an even layer. Bake until the cakes are golden and a toothpick inserted into the centers comes out clean, 40–45 minutes. Transfer the pans to a wire rack and let cool for 15 minutes. Turn the pans over onto the rack. Lift off the pans, peel off the parchment paper, and let the cakes cool completely.

Using a serrated knife, cut each cake layer in half horizontally. Place the bottom of 1 cake layer on a cake stand or plate. Using an offset spatula, spread some of the frosting over the top, making a thin, even layer. Place a second cake layer, cut side down, on top of the frosting, lining up the sides of the cakes. Spread more frosting over the top. Repeat with the remaining 2 layers. Spread a thick layer of the remaining frosting over the cake top. Smooth the frosting around the sides with the spatula so that the sides of the cake are peeking through. Cut the cake into wedges and serve.

warm molten chocolate cakes

There's a reason why these cakes stand the test of time—plunge a spoon into one and you'll find gooey chocolate bliss. Dress them up with sliced poached pears (page 142) or marinated blood-orange segments (page 125) and a dollop of crème fraîche, or serve them with scoops of vanilla ice cream. In summer, garnish with fresh berries.

8 oz (225 g) bittersweet chocolate, finely chopped

¼ cup (2 oz/60 g) unsalted butter, cut into pieces, plus more for greasing

1 teaspoon vanilla extract

¼ teaspoon salt

3 large eggs, separated, plus 1 large egg yolk

6 tablespoons (3 oz/80 g) sugar

2 tablespoons unsweetened natural cocoa powder, sifted, plus more for dusting

MAKES 6 SERVINGS

Preheat the oven to 400°F (200°C). Lightly grease six ¾-cup (180-ml) ramekins, then dust with cocoa, tapping out any excess. Set the ramekins on a small baking sheet.

Place the chocolate and butter in a heatproof bowl set over but not touching barely simmering water in a saucepan and melt the chocolate, whisking until the mixture is glossy and smooth. Remove the bowl from the pan and stir in the vanilla and salt. Set aside to cool slightly.

In a large bowl, using an electric mixer on medium-high speed, beat together the 4 egg yolks, 3 tablespoons of the sugar, and the cocoa until thick. Add the melted chocolate mixture to the yolk mixture and beat until blended. The mixture will be very thick.

In a bowl, using clean beaters, beat the 3 egg whites on medium-high speed until very foamy and thick, about 3 minutes. Raise the speed to high, sprinkle in the remaining 3 tablespoons sugar, and continue beating until firm, glossy peaks form. Spoon half of the beaten whites onto the chocolate mixture and stir just until blended. Gently fold in the remaining whites. Divide the batter evenly among the prepared ramekins.

Bake until the cakes are puffed and the tops are cracked, about 13 minutes. The inside of the cracks will look very wet. Remove from the oven and serve. Or, run a small knife around the inside of each ramekin and invert the cakes onto plates.

chocolate babka

Babka is a sweet yeasted bread that hails from Eastern European Jewish traditions, and often contains chocolate, cinnamon, or apple fillings. Rolling and twisting the filled dough, in this case chocolate and cinnamon, results in gorgeous swirls. Serve the bread when still warm or lightly toast and butter slices the next day.

FOR THE DOUGH

¾ cup (180 ml) warm whole milk (105°–115°F/40°–46°C)

1 tablespoon honey

1 package (2¼ teaspoons) active dry yeast

2¼ cups (10 oz/270 g) all-purpose flour, plus more for dusting

1 large egg

1 teaspoon salt

½ cup (4 oz/115 g) unsalted butter, at cool room temperature, plus more for greasing

FOR THE FILLING

¾ cup (1½ oz/130 g) mini semisweet chocolate chips

¼ cup (¾ oz/20 g) unsweetened cocoa powder

¼ cup (1¾ oz/50 g) sugar

¼ teaspoon ground cinnamon

¼ cup (2 oz/60 g) unsalted butter, melted and cooled

1 large egg, beaten with 1 teaspoon water

MAKES 10–12 SERVINGS

To make the dough, in the bowl of a stand mixer, stir together the milk, honey, yeast, and ¼ cup (1 oz/30 g) of the flour. Let stand until frothy, about 10 minutes.

Fit the stand mixer with the dough hook attachment. Add the remaining 2 cups (9 oz/240 g) flour, the egg, and the salt to the yeast mixture in the bowl. Beat on low speed until the ingredients start to come together. Add the butter a few tablespoons at a time, and beat on medium speed until incorporated, turning off the mixer and scraping down the sides of the bowl as needed. The dough will start out very shaggy but should become soft and slightly sticky after about 4 minutes. Continue to beat on medium speed for about 5 minutes longer.

Grease a large bowl. Form the dough into a ball, place in the bowl, and turn to coat with the butter. Cover with plastic wrap and let rise in a warm spot until doubled in size, about 1½ hours.

To make the filling, in a food processor, combine the chocolate chips, cocoa powder, sugar, and cinnamon. Process until well combined and the chips are chopped fairly small. Add the melted butter and process to a thick paste. Set aside.

Grease a 9-by-5-inch (23-by-13-cm) loaf pan with butter. Line with parchment paper, letting the paper overhang the long edges of the pan by 1 or 2 inches (2.5 or 5 cm).

Sprinkle a work surface with flour. Transfer the dough to the floured surface. Using a rolling pin, roll out the dough into a 10-by-12-inch (25-by-30-cm) rectangle, with a long edge facing you. Gently spread the chocolate filling over the dough in an even layer, taking care not to tear the dough (the filling is thick, so use your fingers to help spread it). Starting with the long edge closest to you, tightly roll up the dough with the filling inside. Cut the dough log in half lengthwise. Position the 2 dough pieces, cut side up, so that they form an X, then twist the ends twice on one side and then on the other. Scrunch the loaf together so it's the length of the loaf pan, then carefully transfer it, cut sides up, to the prepared pan.

Lay a piece of plastic wrap loosely over the top. Let the dough rise in a warm place until doubled in size, about 1 hour.

Preheat the oven to 375°F (190°C).

When the dough has risen, remove the plastic wrap. Gently brush the egg wash over the top of the dough. Bake until golden brown, about 40 minutes. Transfer the pan to a wire rack and let cool for 15 minutes. Turn out the babka and remove the parchment paper, then let cool completely. Cut the babka into slices and serve.

panettone

This tall, lightly sweetened yeast bread is a specialty of Milan, Italy, where it has been popular for centuries. This recipe for the classic version includes golden raisins and candied citrus peel, but variations like chocolate or plain panettone are also common. Serve big wedges of the bread with tea or a glass of sweet Italian wine.

FOR THE SPONGE

¼ cup (60 ml) warm water (105°–115°F/40°–46°C)

⅔ cup (160 ml) warm whole milk (105°–115°F/40°–46°C)

2 packages (4½ teaspoons) active dry yeast

Pinch of granulated sugar

½ cup (2 oz/60 g) bread flour

¾ cup (6 oz/170 g) unsalted butter, melted, plus more for greasing

½ cup (3½ oz/100 g) granulated sugar

Finely grated zest of 1 orange or lemon

1½ teaspoons salt

2 large eggs, plus 3 large egg yolks

3½ cups (15 oz/450 g) bread flour, plus more as needed

1 cup (6 oz/170 g) golden raisins

½ cup (3 oz/90 g) diced candied lemon peel

½ cup (3 oz/90 g) diced candied orange peel

2 tablespoons raw or coarse sugar

MAKES 2 LOAVES

To make the sponge, in the bowl of a stand mixer fitted with the whisk attachment, combine the water and milk. Sprinkle the yeast and granulated sugar over the liquid and stir to dissolve. Let stand until foamy, about 10 minutes. Add the flour and beat on medium speed until smooth. Cover the bowl loosely with plastic wrap and let stand at room temperature for 30 minutes.

Add the butter, granulated sugar, citrus zest, salt, eggs, egg yolks, and 1 cup (4 oz/120 g) of the flour to the sponge and switch to the paddle attachment. Beat on medium speed for 1 minute. Beat in the remaining 2½ cups (11 oz/ 330 g) flour, ½ cup (2 oz/60 g) at a time, until the dough pulls away from the bowl sides. Switch to the dough hook. Knead on low speed, adding flour 1 tablespoon at a time if the dough sticks, until the dough is soft, smooth, and springy, about 5 minutes. Brush a large bowl with melted butter. Transfer the dough to the bowl and turn the dough once to coat it. Cover loosely with plastic wrap and let rise at room temperature until doubled in size, 1½–2 hours.

Turn the dough out onto a lightly floured work surface and knead gently for a minute. Return to the bowl, re-cover, and let rise again at room temperature until doubled in size, about 1 hour.

Grease two 6-by-3-inch (15-cm-by-7.5-cm) round cake or springform pans, line the bottoms with parchment paper, then grease the paper. Tie a strip of buttered aluminum foil around the outside of each pan with kitchen string, making a collar that extends 2–3 inches (5–7.5 cm) above the rim of the pan.

Turn the dough out onto a lightly floured work surface. In a small bowl, stir together the raisins and candied lemon and orange peel. Pat the dough into a large oval and sprinkle evenly with half of the fruit mixture. Press into the dough to adhere and roll the dough up. Pat again into an oval, sprinkle evenly with the remaining fruit, and press to adhere. Roll the dough up again. Knead a few times to smooth out the dough. Divide the dough in half and shape into 2 tight round loaves, gently pulling the surface taut from the bottom. Place each dough ball in a prepared pan. Cover loosely with plastic wrap and let rise at room temperature until the dough comes up to the rim of the foil collar, about 1½ hours.

Place a baking stone on the center oven rack and preheat to 400°F (200°C). Sprinkle the top of each loaf with half of the raw sugar.

Place the pans on the stone and bake for 10 minutes. Reduce the oven temperature to 350°F (180°C) and bake until the loaves are golden brown and a toothpick inserted into the center of each loaf comes out clean, 25–30 minutes longer. Transfer the pans to wire racks and let the breads cool in the pans for 5 minutes, then remove the foil collars. Gently turn the breads out onto the racks. Turn right side up and let cool completely before slicing and serving.

basics

sugar cookies

1¼ cups (10 oz/285 g) unsalted butter, at cool room temperature

¾ cup (5 oz/140 g) sugar

1 large egg yolk

2 teaspoons vanilla extract

2 cups (9 oz/240 g) all-purpose flour

¼ teaspoon salt

MAKES ABOUT 36 COOKIES

In a large bowl, using an electric mixer on medium-high speed, beat the butter and sugar until fluffy and pale, about 3 minutes. Beat in the egg yolk and vanilla until well blended. Reduce the speed to low, sift the flour and salt over the butter mixture, and mix just until blended. Divide the dough into 4 equal portions. Shape into disks, wrap in plastic wrap, and refrigerate for at least 2 hours or up to overnight.

Preheat the oven to 350°F (180°C). Line 2 baking sheets with parchment paper. Let the dough stand at room temperature for 15 minutes. Roll out each disk between 2 sheets of parchment paper to about ¼ inch (6 mm) thick. Using cookie cutters, cut out cookies. Gather up the scraps, press them together, reroll, and cut out more shapes. If the scraps become sticky, refrigerate them for 10 minutes before rerolling. If using an intricately shaped cutter, refrigerate the cutout cookies for 15–30 minutes before baking.

Transfer the cookies to the prepared baking sheets. Bake until lightly golden on the bottom, 10–12 minutes. Transfer the baking sheets to wire racks and let cool briefly on the sheets before transferring the cookies to the racks to cool completely.

NOTE *Top these cookies with decorating sugar or sprinkles before baking, or ice with a thick coat of Vanilla Icing (page 170) then top with sprinkles. Or you can pipe decorations on using Royal Icing (page 170) for an elegant touch.*

chocolate sugar cookies

2¼ cups (10 oz/270 g) all-purpose flour

⅓ cup (1 oz/30 g) unsweetened cocoa powder

½ teaspoon baking powder

½ teaspoon baking soda

¼ teaspoon salt

¾ cup (6 oz/170 g) unsalted butter, at cool room temperature

1 cup (7½ oz/210 g) firmly packed light brown sugar

¼ cup (1¾ oz/50 g) granulated sugar

1 large egg

1 teaspoon vanilla extract

MAKES ABOUT 36 COOKIES

In a bowl, sift together the flour, cocoa powder, baking powder, baking soda, and salt. Set aside. In a large bowl, using an electric mixer on medium-high speed, beat together the butter, brown sugar, and granulated sugar until light and fluffy, about 3 minutes. Reduce the speed to low, add the egg and vanilla, and beat until combined, about 1 minute. Stop the mixer and scrape down the sides of the bowl. Add the flour mixture and beat on low speed until combined, about 1 minute. Divide the dough into 4 equal portions. Shape into disks, wrap in plastic wrap, and refrigerate for at least 2 hours or up to overnight.

Preheat the oven to 350°F (180°C). Line 2 baking sheets with parchment paper. Let the dough stand at room temperature for 15 minutes. Roll out each disk between 2 sheets of parchment paper to about ¼ inch (6 mm) thick. Using cookie cutters, cut out shapes. Gather up the dough scraps, press them together, roll out, and cut out more cookies. If the scraps are sticky, refrigerate them for 10 minutes before rerolling. If using an intricately shaped cutter, refrigerate the cutout cookies for 15–30 minutes before baking.

Transfer the cutouts to the prepared baking sheets. Bake until firm to the touch, about 12 minutes. Transfer the baking sheets to wire racks and let cool briefly before transferring the cookies to the racks to cool completely.

NOTE *Top these cookies with decorating sugar or sprinkles before baking, or ice with a thick coat of Vanilla Icing (page 170) then top with sprinkles. Or you can pipe decorations on using Royal Icing (page 170) for an elegant touch.*

flaky pie dough, single crust

1¼ cups (5½ oz/155 g) all-purpose flour

2 teaspoons sugar (optional)

¼ teaspoon salt

7 tablespoons (3½ oz/105 g) cold unsalted butter, cut into pieces

5 tablespoons (75 ml) ice-cold water, plus more if needed

MAKES ONE 9-INCH (23-CM) SINGLE CRUST

In a food processor, combine the flour, sugar, if using, and salt. Sprinkle the butter over the top and pulse for a few seconds, just until the butter is the size of small peas. Sprinkle the water evenly over the flour mixture, then process just until the mixture starts to come together. Dump the dough into a large zippered plastic bag and press into a flat disk. Refrigerate for at least 30 minutes or up to 1 day before using, or freeze for up to 1 month.

flaky pie dough, double crust

2½ cups (11 oz/310 g) all-purpose flour

1 tablespoon sugar (optional)

½ teaspoon salt

¾ cup (6 oz/170 g) cold unsalted butter, cut into pieces

⅔ cup (160 ml) ice-cold water, plus more if needed

MAKES ONE 9-INCH (23-CM) DOUBLE CRUST

In a food processor, combine the flour, sugar, if using, and salt. Sprinkle the butter over the top and pulse for a few seconds, just until the butter is the size of small peas. Sprinkle the water evenly over the flour mixture, then process just until the mixture starts to come together. Dump the dough into a large zippered plastic bag and press into a flat disk. Refrigerate for at least 30 minutes or up to 1 day before using, or freeze for up to 1 month.

tart dough

1 large egg yolk

2 tablespoons very cold water

1 teaspoon vanilla extract

1½ cups (6½ oz/180 g) all-purpose flour

⅓ cup (2½ oz/70 g) sugar

¼ teaspoon salt

½ cup (4 oz/115 g) cold unsalted butter, cut into ¼-inch (6-mm) cubes

MAKES ONE 9½-INCH (24-CM) TART OR SIX 4-INCH (10-CM) TARTLETS

In a small bowl, whisk together the egg yolk, water, and vanilla. Set aside.

In a food processor, combine the flour, sugar, and salt. Sprinkle the butter over the top and pulse for a few seconds, just until the butter is the size of small peas. Add the egg mixture to the flour mixture, then process just until the mixture starts to come together. Dump the dough into a large zippered plastic bag and press into a flat disk. Refrigerate for at least 30 minutes or up to 1 day before using, or freeze for up to 1 month.

cocoa tart dough

½ cup (4 oz/115 g) unsalted butter, at cool room temperature, cut into pieces

⅓ cup (1⅓ oz/40 g) confectioners' sugar, sifted

1 large egg yolk

1 teaspoon vanilla extract

¼ teaspoon salt

1¼ cups (5½ oz/155 g) all-purpose flour

¼ cup (¾ oz/20 g) cocoa powder

MAKES ONE 9½-INCH (24-CM) TART OR TWELVE 2-INCH (5-CM) TARTLETS

In a large bowl, using an electric mixer on medium-low speed, beat together the butter, sugar, egg yolk, vanilla, and salt until smooth and creamy, about 1 minute. Turn off the mixer and scrape down the sides of the bowl. Reduce the speed to low, sift together the flour and cocoa powder over the butter mixture, and beat just until the mixture is evenly moistened and starts to clump together, about 1 minute. If the dough seems dry, add a little water 1 teaspoon at a time until it comes together. Dump the dough onto a clean work surface and press into a thick disk. Wrap the disk in plastic wrap and refrigerate for at least 30 minutes or up to overnight before using.

cream cheese tartlet dough

½ cup (4 oz/115 g) unsalted butter, at cool room temperature

3 oz (85 g) cream cheese

1 cup (4¼ oz/120 g) all-purpose flour, sifted

MAKES ONE 9½-INCH (24-CM) TART OR SIX 4-INCH (10-CM) TARTLETS

In the bowl of a stand mixer fitted with the paddle attachment, beat the butter and cream cheese on low speed until smooth and blended, about 45 seconds. Add the flour and mix until a smooth dough forms. Transfer the dough to a work surface and shape into a thick log. Wrap with plastic wrap and store in the refrigerator until ready to use, up to 3 days.

wafer cookie crust

2 cups (8 oz) chocolate or vanilla wafer cookies

2 tablespoons sugar

¼ teaspoon salt

6 tablespoons (3 oz/90 g) unsalted butter, melted and cooled

MAKES ONE 9-INCH (23-CM) CRUST

Preheat the oven to 350°F (180°C). In a food processor, pulse the cookies until fine crumbs form. Add the sugar and salt and pulse a few times to mix evenly. Add the butter and pulse until the texture resembles wet sand. Gently press the mixture evenly into the bottom and up the sides of a 9-inch (23-cm) pie dish, pressing until compact. Bake until the crust is set, about 10 minutes. Let cool completely on a wire rack before filling. (If the sides slump during baking, gently press the crust back up the sides once the crust is still very warm but cool enough to handle.)

gingersnap crust

4 cups (1 lb/450 g)
gingersnap cookies

3 tablespoons sugar

½ teaspoon salt

½ cup (4 oz/115 g) unsalted
butter, melted and cooled

**MAKES ONE 9-INCH
(23-CM) CRUST**

Preheat the oven to 350°F (180°C). In a food processor, process the gingersnap cookies until fine crumbs form. Add the sugar and salt and pulse a few times to mix. Add the butter and pulse until the texture resembles wet sand. Gently press the mixture evenly into the bottom and up the sides of a 9-inch (23-cm) pie dish, pressing until compact. Bake until the crust is set, about 10 minutes. Let cool completely on a wire rack before filling.

chocolate ganache

1 cup (250 ml) heavy cream

1 tablespoon light corn syrup

Pinch of salt

8 oz (225 g) semisweet
chocolate, chopped

**MAKES ABOUT 1¾ CUPS
(190 ML)**

In a medium saucepan over medium-high heat, stir together the cream, corn syrup, and salt. Bring to a simmer, then remove from the heat. Add the chocolate and let stand for about 3 minutes. Stir until the chocolate is completely melted and the mixture is smooth. Let cool until warm if using the ganache as a filling; let cool to room temperature if using as a topping or frosting. The cooled ganache can be refrigerated in an airtight container for up to 3 days. Before using, soften the ganache by gently heating it in a heatproof bowl set over but not touching simmering water in a saucepan.

vanilla icing

2 cups (8 oz/230 g) confectioners' sugar, sifted

1–3 tablespoons whole milk, or as needed

1 teaspoon vanilla extract

MAKES ABOUT 1 CUP (250 ML)

In a bowl, whisk together the' sugar, 1 tablespoon milk, and vanilla until smooth. If the mixture is too thick, add more milk 1 teaspoon at a time to achieve the desired consistency. Whisk until smooth. Store in an airtight container at room temperature overnight or in the refrigerator for up to 3 days. If refrigerated, let stand at room temperature for about 1 hour before using.

royal icing

WITH EGG

3 large egg whites, at room temperature

¼ teaspoon cream of tartar

4 cups (1 lb/460 g) confectioners' sugar, sifted

WITHOUT EGG

3 tablespoons meringue powder

6 tablespoons (90 ml) warm water, plus more as needed

4 cups (1 lb/460 g) confectioners' sugar, sifted

MAKES ABOUT 2 CUPS (500 ML)

To make royal icing with egg, in a large bowl, using an electric mixer on medium speed, beat the egg whites and cream of tartar until foamy, about 2 minutes. Reduce the speed to low and gradually beat in the sugar until blended, then beat on high speed until thick and glossy, about 2 minutes.

To make royal icing without egg, in a large bowl, using an electric mixer on medium speed, beat together the meringue powder and warm water. Reduce the speed to low and gradually beat in the sugar until blended, then beat on high speed until very thick and smooth, about 5 minutes.

Beat in more warm water, 1 tablespoon at a time, if the icing is too thick to spread or pipe.

fluffy vanilla frosting

½ cup (4 oz/115 g) unsalted butter, at room temperature

2½ cups (10 oz/290 g) confectioners' sugar, sifted

3 tablespoons whole milk

1 teaspoon vanilla extract

Pinch of salt

MAKES ENOUGH FOR ONE 9-INCH (23-CM) LAYER CAKE

In a large bowl, using an electric mixer on medium speed, beat the butter until light and fluffy, about 2 minutes. Add the sugar, milk, vanilla, and salt, reduce the speed to low, and mix just until combined. Stop the mixer and scrape down the sides of the bowl. Raise the speed to medium-high and beat until the frosting is airy and smooth, about 5 minutes. Store in an airtight container at room temperature overnight or in the refrigerator for up to 3 days. If refrigerated, let stand at room temperature for about 1 hour before using.

fudge frosting

1 cup (8 oz/225 g) unsalted butter, at cool room temperature

2½ cups (10 oz/290 g) confectioners' sugar, sifted

2 teaspoons vanilla extract

8 oz (240 g) unsweetened chocolate, melted and cooled

MAKES ENOUGH FOR ONE 9-INCH (23-CM) LAYER CAKE

In a large bowl, using an electric mixer on medium-high speed, beat the butter until fluffy, about 3 minutes. Add the sugar and beat until light and fluffy, about 2 minutes. Beat in the vanilla. Reduce the speed to low, add the cooled chocolate, and beat until incorporated, then increase the speed and beat until light and fluffy, about 2 minutes. Store in an airtight container at room temperature overnight or in the refrigerator for up to 3 days. If refrigerated, let stand at room temperature for about 1 hour before using.

chocolate frosting

4 cups (1 lb/460 g) confectioners' sugar, sifted

1 cup (3 oz/90 g) unsweetened cocoa powder

½ cup (4 oz/115 g) unsalted butter, at cool room temperature

1 teaspoon vanilla extract

1 cup (250 ml) heavy cream, plus more if needed

MAKES ENOUGH FOR ONE 9-INCH (23-CM) LAYER CAKE, 12 CUPCAKES, OR 24 MINI CUPCAKES

In a large bowl, sift together the sugar and cocoa powder. Using an electric mixer on low speed, mix in the butter until the mixture looks like fine bread crumbs. Mix in the vanilla and then gradually beat in the cream to make a spreadable frosting, adding more cream by the tablespoon if needed. Raise the speed to high and beat until the frosting is smooth and fluffy, about 3 minutes. Store in an airtight container at room temperature overnight or in the refrigerator for up to 3 days. If refrigerated, let stand at room temperature for about 1 hour before using.

white chocolate frosting

½ cup (4 oz/115 g) unsalted butter, at cool room temperature

2½ cups (10 oz/290 g) confectioners' sugar

3 tablespoons milk

½ teaspoon vanilla extract

Pinch of salt

4 oz (110 g) white chocolate, finely chopped and melted

MAKES ENOUGH FOR ONE 9-INCH (23-CM) LAYER CAKE, 12 CUPCAKES, OR 24 MINI CUPCAKES

In a large bowl, using an electric mixer on medium speed, beat the butter until light and fluffy, about 2 minutes. Add the sugar, milk, vanilla, and salt and beat until combined. Add the white chocolate and beat until combined. Stop the mixer and scrape down the sides of the bowl. Raise the speed to medium-high and beat until the frosting is fluffy and smooth, about 5 minutes. Store in an airtight container in the refrigerator for up to 3 days. If refrigerated, let stand at room temperature for about 1 hour before using.

White Chocolate–Peppermint Frosting

Replace the vanilla with ½ teaspoon peppermint extract.

cream cheese frosting

12 oz (375 g) cream cheese, at cool room temperature

6 tablespoons (3 oz/90 g) unsalted butter, at cool room temperature

2 teaspoons vanilla extract

1½ cups (6 oz/185 g) confectioners' sugar, sifted

MAKES ENOUGH FOR ONE 9-BY-13-INCH (23-BY-33 CM) CAKE, A 9-INCH (23-CM) LAYER CAKE, 12 CUPCAKES, OR 24 MINI CUPCAKES

In a large bowl, using an electric mixer on medium-high speed, beat the cream cheese, butter, and vanilla until light and fluffy, about 2 minutes. Gradually beat in the sugar and continue to mix until thoroughly combined, stopping the mixer and scraping down the sides of the bowl as needed. Use right away, or, if the consistency is too soft, refrigerate the frosting until it is spreadable, 10–15 minutes. The frosting will keep in the refrigerator for up to 3 days.

whipped honey frosting

1 cup (8 oz/225 g) unsalted butter, at room temperature

⅓ cup (115 g) honey

¼ teaspoon salt

4 cups (1 lb/460 g) confectioners' sugar, sifted

3 tablespoons heavy cream, plus more as needed

2 teaspoons vanilla extract

MAKES ABOUT 2½ CUPS (375 ML)

In a large bowl, using an electric mixer on medium-high speed, beat the butter, honey, and salt until light and fluffy, about 2 minutes. Turn off the mixer and scrape down the sides of the bowl. Reduce the speed to low, sift 2 cups (8 oz/225 g) of the sugar into the bowl, and beat until the sugar is incorporated. Raise the speed to medium-high and beat until smooth, about 3 minutes. Sift the remaining 2 cups (8 oz/230 g) sugar into the bowl, add the cream and vanilla, and beat on low speed until incorporated. Scrape down the sides of the bowl. Beat on medium-high speed until the frosting is fluffy and smooth, about 5 minutes. The frosting should be easily spreadable; if not, add more cream 1 tablespoon at a time until the desired consistency is reached. Use right away, or store in an airtight container in the refrigerator for up to 2 days. Stir vigorously just before using.

quick vanilla buttercream

2 cups (1 lb/450 g)
unsalted butter, at cool
room temperature

3 cups (12 oz/345 g)
confectioners' sugar, sifted

2 teaspoons vanilla extract

⅛ teaspoon salt

**MAKES ENOUGH FOR ONE
9-INCH (23-CM) LAYER CAKE**

In a large bowl, using an electric mixer on medium speed, beat the butter until smooth, about 2 minutes. Add the sugar, vanilla, and salt. Raise the speed to medium-high and beat until well combined, stopping the mixer and scraping down the sides of the bowl as needed. Store the buttercream in an airtight container at room temperature overnight or in the refrigerator for up to 3 days. If refrigerated, let stand at room temperature for about 1 hour before frosting your cake.

vanilla meringue buttercream

3 large egg whites

1 cup (7 oz/200 g) sugar

1 cup (8 oz/225 g)
unsalted butter, at cool
room temperature

1 teaspoon vanilla extract

**MAKES ENOUGH FOR ONE
9-INCH (23-CM) LAYER CAKE**

Combine the egg whites and sugar in the bowl of a stand mixer and set the bowl over but not touching barely simmering water in a saucepan. Whisking constantly, warm the mixture until it is hot to the touch, registering about 160°F (71°C) on a candy thermometer.

Attach the bowl to the stand mixer fitted with the whisk attachment and beat on medium-high speed until the mixture reaches room temperature, about 15 minutes. Add the butter a few tablespoons at a time, and beat on low speed until incorporated. Beat in the vanilla. If the buttercream becomes grainy, raise the speed to high and beat until smooth, 1–3 minutes. Store the buttercream in an airtight container in the refrigerator for up to 3 days. If refrigerated, let stand at room temperature for about 1 hour to soften before using.

coconut buttercream

1 cup (8 oz/225 g) unsalted butter, at cool room temperature

½ cup (120 ml) coconut milk

4 cups (1 lb/460 g) confectioners' sugar, sifted

½ teaspoon vanilla extract

½ teaspoon coconut extract

⅛ teaspoon salt

MAKES ENOUGH FOR ONE 8-INCH (20-CM) 3-LAYER CAKE

In a large bowl, using an electric mixer on medium speed, beat the butter and coconut milk until smooth, about 2 minutes. Add the sugar, vanilla, coconut extract, and salt. Raise the speed to medium-high and beat until well combined, stopping the mixer and scraping down the sides of the bowl as needed. Store the buttercream in an airtight container at room temperature overnight or in the refrigerator for up to 3 days. If refrigerated, let stand at room temperature for about 1 hour before using.

mocha buttercream

8 oz (225 g) bittersweet chocolate, chopped

¼ cup (60 ml) strong brewed coffee

4 large egg yolks

1 cup (7 oz/200 g) sugar

1½ cups (12 oz/340 g) unsalted butter, at cool room temperature, cut into pieces

3 tablespoons dark rum

MAKES ENOUGH FOR ONE 9-INCH (23-CM) LAYER CAKE

Place the chocolate and coffee in a heatproof bowl set over but not touching barely simmering water in a saucepan, and heat until the chocolate melts. Remove the bowl from the pan and keep warm. Place the egg yolks in another heatproof bowl set over but not touching the simmering water, and whisk for a few minutes until warm. Remove the bowl from the pan and beat the yolks on high speed until thick and pale.

In a small saucepan over high heat, bring the sugar and ⅓ cup (80 ml) water to a boil, stirring until the sugar dissolves. Boil rapidly until the sugar registers 236°F (113°C) on a candy thermometer. With the mixer on low speed, gradually beat the hot syrup into the beaten yolks. Fold in the chocolate mixture. Beat in the butter a little at a time. Beat in the rum. Refrigerate until the buttercream is thick enough to spread.

whipped cream

1 cup (250 ml) heavy cream

2 tablespoons sugar

½ teaspoon vanilla extract

MAKES ABOUT 2 CUPS (500 ML)

In a bowl, using an electric mixer on medium speed, whip the cream, sugar, and vanilla until medium peaks form. Use right away or cover with plastic wrap and refrigerate until ready to use, up to 4 hours. Whisk the cream briefly before using.

vanilla bean pastry cream

1 cup (250 ml) heavy cream

2½ cups (625 ml) whole milk

1 vanilla bean

6 large egg yolks

½ cup (3½ oz/100 g) sugar

Pinch of salt

3 tablespoons cornstarch, mixed with 2 tablespoons water

MAKES ENOUGH FOR 1 LARGE TRIFLE, ONE 10-INCH (24-CM) TART, OR ONE 9-INCH (23-CM) PIE

In a medium saucepan over low heat, warm the cream and milk. Split the vanilla bean and scrape out the seeds with the back of a paring knife. Add the pod and seeds to the warm cream mixture. In another bowl, whisk together the egg yolks, sugar, and salt, then stir in the cornstarch mixture. Slowly pour about half of the warm cream mixture into the yolk mixture, whisking constantly. Pour the yolk mixture into the saucepan and raise the heat to medium-low. Cook, stirring constantly, until the custard is thickened, about 4 minutes. Strain through a medium-mesh sieve into a bowl. Press plastic wrap directly onto the surface of the custard and let cool completely before using, at least 2 hours or up to 3 days.

lemon curd

1 large egg plus 4 large
egg yolks

½ cup (3½ oz/100 g) sugar

⅓ cup (80 ml) resh lemon
juice, strained

2 tablespoons unsalted butter

MAKES ⅔ CUP (160 ML)

Place the egg, egg yolks, sugar, and lemon juice in a heatproof bowl set over but not touching barely simmering water in a saucepan, and whisk together. Cook, stirring constantly, until thickened, about 5 minutes. Remove the bowl from the heat and add the butter, stirring until incorporated. Strain the lemon curd through a fine-mesh sieve into another bowl. Press plastic wrap directly onto the surface of the curd and refrigerate until chilled, at least 2 hours or up to 3 days.

Meyer Lemon Curd

Substitute an equal amount of Meyer lemon juice, plus zest, for the lemon.

lime curd

8 large egg yolks

1½ cups (10½ oz/300 g) sugar

2 tablespoons finely grated
lime zest

¾ cup (180 ml) fresh
lime juice

¾ cup (6 oz/170 g)
cold unsalted butter,
cut into pieces

MAKES 1 CUP (250 ML)

In a saucepan over medium heat, combine the egg yolks, sugar, and lime zest and juice. Cook, whisking often, until the mixture is thick enough to coat the back of a spoon, about 10 minutes. Add the butter and cook, stirring often, until melted, about 3 minutes. Reduce the heat to low and cook, whisking constantly, until the mixture starts to thicken, about 1 minute longer. Strain the lime curd through a fine-mesh sieve into a bowl. Press plastic wrap directly onto the surface of the curd and refrigerate until chilled, at least 2 hours or up to 3 days.

index

a

Alfajores, Dulce de Leche, 59
Almonds
 Almond Cookies, 126
 Almond-Jam Cakes, 110
 Apricot-Almond Crisp, 66
 Apricot Mascarpone Crostata, 33
 Bittersweet Chocolate Almond
  Torte, 49
 Caramel Cranberry-Almond
  Tart, 99
 Chestnut Torte with Mocha
  Buttercream, 140
 Chocolate, Raspberry & Toasted
  Almond Bark, 133
 Chocolate-Dipped Coconut-
  Almond Macaroons, 20
 Chocolate Florentines, 155
 Honey-Nectarine Cheesecake, 74
 Mexican Wedding Cookies, 23
 Pear-Almond Custard Tart, 142–43
 Raspberry Linzer Heart
  Cookies, 138
 Summer Peach-Raspberry
  Muffins, 80
Angel Food Cake with Strawberry-
 Rhubarb Compote, 50–51

Apples, 13
 Apple-Ginger Tart with Cider-
  Bourbon Sauce, 104
 Classic Tarte Tatin, 107
 Spiced Apple Strudel, 146
Applesauce
 Spiced Apple Honey Cake, 156
Apricots
 Apricot-Almond Crisp, 66
 Apricot Mascarpone Crostata, 33
 Apricot-Pistachio Rugelach, 22
 Spiced Apple Strudel, 146

b

Babka, Chocolate, 158–59
Baking tips, 14
Baklava, Honey Pistachio, 69
Bark, Chocolate, Raspberry &
 Toasted Almond, 133
Bars
 Blueberry Cheesecake Squares
  with Hazelnut Crust, 64
 Lime Curd Coconut Bars, 61
 Peppermint Bark Brownies, 128
 Plum Jam Oatmeal Streusel
  Bars, 62
Beignets, 30

Berries, 13. *See also* Cranberries;
 Raspberries; Strawberries
 Berries & Cream Roulade, 89
 Blackberry Cobbler, 56
 Blueberry Cheesecake Squares
  with Hazelnut Crust, 64
 Blueberry-Lemon Drizzle Cake, 75
Biscotti, Chocolate, Cherry &
 Hazelnut, 101
Bittersweet Chocolate Almond
 Torte, 49
Bittersweet Chocolate & Salted
 Caramel Tart, 145
Blackberry Cobbler, 56
Blood Orange Tartlets, 147
Blueberry Cheesecake Squares with
 Hazelnut Crust, 64
Blueberry-Lemon Drizzle Cake, 75
Bourbon
 Apple-Ginger Tart with Cider-
  Bourbon Sauce, 104
 Butterscotch-Bourbon Pie, 109
Bread
 Bread & Butter Pudding with
  Marmalade, 114
 Challah, 119
 Chocolate Babka, 158–59
 Panettone, 160–61
 Sweet Potato Corn Bread, 115

Brittle, Pistachio, 96
Brownies, Peppermint Bark, 128
Bûche de Noël, Mocha, 151
Buns, Hot Cross, 26
Butterscotch-Bourbon Pie, 109

C

Cakes. *See also* Cupcakes
  Angel Food Cake with
    Strawberry-Rhubarb
    Compote, 50–51
  Berries & Cream Roulade, 89
  Bittersweet Chocolate Almond
    Torte, 49
  Blueberry-Lemon Drizzle
    Cake, 75
  Caramelized Pear Ginger
    Cake, 94
  Carrot Cake, 52
  Chestnut Torte with Mocha
    Buttercream, 140
  Chocolate Espresso Heart
    Cake, 150
  Chocolate Mint Chip Ice Cream
    Cake, 79
  Coconut Lime Curd Layer
    Cake, 42–43
  Cranberry Upside-Down
    Cake, 117
  King Cake, 53
  Mocha Bûche de Noël, 151
  Orange Vanilla Bean Sponge
    Cake with Sugared
    Strawberries, 47

Pumpkin Coffee Cake with Pecan
    Streusel, 118
  Red, White & Blue Bundt Cake, 87
  Rose & Vanilla Tea Cakes, 27
  Spiced Apple Honey Cake, 156
  Strawberry-Rhubarb Breakfast
    Cake, 35
  Tres Leches Cake, 86
  Triple-Decker Birthday Cake, 88
  Vanilla Ombré Layer Cake, 82–83
  Warm Molten Chocolate
    Cakes, 157
Caramel
  Bittersweet Chocolate & Salted
    Caramel Tart, 145
  Caramel Cranberry-Almond
    Tart, 99
  Caramel Orange Flan, 63
Caramelized Pear Ginger Cake, 94
Carrot Cake, 52
Challah, 119
Cheese. *See also* Cream cheese
  Apricot Mascarpone Crostata, 33
Cheesecake, Honey-Nectarine, 74
Cheesecake Cupcakes,
    Strawberry, 39
Cheesecake Squares, Blueberry,
    with Hazelnut Crust, 64
Cherries
  Cherry Clafoutis, 31
  Cherry Lattice Pie, 71
  Chocolate, Cherry & Hazelnut
    Biscotti, 101
  Sour Cherry Pot Pies, 36
  Spiced Apple Strudel, 146
Chestnut Torte with Mocha
  Buttercream, 140

Chocolate. *See also*
  White chocolate
  Bittersweet Chocolate Almond
    Torte, 49
  Bittersweet Chocolate & Salted
    Caramel Tart, 145
  Chocolate, Cherry & Hazelnut
    Biscotti, 101
  Chocolate, Raspberry & Toasted
    Almond Bark, 133
  Chocolate Babka, 158–59
  Chocolate-Dipped Coconut-
    Almond Macaroons, 20
  Chocolate Espresso Heart
    Cake, 150
  Chocolate Florentines, 155
  Chocolate Frosting, 172
  Chocolate Ganache, 169
  Chocolate-Hazelnut Pastry
    Wreath, 137
  Chocolate Mint Chip Ice Cream
    Cake, 79
  Chocolate-Raspberry Mini
    Tarts, 135
  Chocolate Sugar Cookies, 165
  Cocoa Tart Dough, 167
  Devil's Food Chocolate
    Cupcakes, 112
  Fudge Frosting, 171
  Honey-Nut Pie, 106
  Hot Cocoa Cookies, 127
  Mocha Bûche de Noël, 151
  Mocha Buttercream, 175
  Peppermint Bark Brownies, 128
  Pumpkin Chocolate Chip
    Cupcakes, 111
  S'mores Fudge, 136

Triple-Decker Birthday Cake, 88
Warm Molten Chocolate
    Cakes, 157
White Chocolate Grasshopper
    Pie, 103
Churros, Cinnamon-Sugar, 72
Cider-Bourbon Sauce, Apple-
    Ginger Tart with, 104
Cinnamon Rolls, 120
Cinnamon-Sugar Churros, 72
Citrus, 13
Clafoutis, Cherry, 31
Classic Pecan Pie, 102
Classic Tarte Tatin, 107
Cobbler, Blackberry, 56
Cocoa Tart Dough, 167
Coconut
    Chocolate-Dipped Coconut-
        Almond Macaroons, 20
    Coconut Buttercream, 175
    Coconut Lime Curd Layer
        Cake, 42–43
    Lime Curd Coconut Bars, 61
    Passion Fruit Cupcakes with
        Coconut Frosting, 44–46
Coffee Cake, Pumpkin, with Pecan
    Streusel, 118
Cookie crusts
    Gingersnap Crust, 169
    Wafer Cookie Crust, 168
Cookies
    Almond Cookies, 126
    Apricot-Pistachio Rugelach, 22
    Chocolate, Cherry & Hazelnut
        Biscotti, 101
    Chocolate-Dipped Coconut-
        Almond Macaroons, 20

Chocolate Florentines, 155
Chocolate Sugar Cookies, 165
Dulce de Leche Alfajores, 59
Gingerbread Cutout Cookies, 132
Hot Cocoa Cookies, 127
Lavender Shortbread, 18
Lemon Crinkle Cookies, 58
Mexican Wedding Cookies, 23
Peppermint Swirl
    Macarons, 130–31
Raspberry Linzer Heart
    Cookies, 138
Strawberry-Pecan
    Thumbprints, 19
Sugar Cookies, 164
Corn Bread, Sweet Potato, 115
Cranberries
    Caramel Cranberry-Almond
        Tart, 99
    Cranberry Upside-Down Cake, 117
    Spiced Apple Strudel, 146
Cream, Whipped, 176
Cream cheese
    Apricot Mascarpone Crostata, 33
    Apricot-Pistachio Rugelach, 22
    Blueberry Cheesecake Squares
        with Hazelnut Crust, 64
    Cream Cheese Frosting, 173
    Cream Cheese Tartlet Dough, 168
    Honey-Nectarine Cheesecake, 74
    Mini Red Velvet Cupcakes with
        Cream Cheese Frosting, 38
    Pumpkin Whoopie Pies, 93
    Spring Strawberry Tart with
        Orange Cream, 34
    Strawberry Cheesecake
        Cupcakes, 39

Crème Brûlée Tartlets, 41
Crisps
    Apricot-Almond Crisp, 66
    Oatmeal Pear Crisp, 95
Crostata, Apricot Mascarpone, 33
Cupcakes
    Almond-Jam Cakes, 110
    Devil's Food Chocolate
        Cupcakes, 112
    Mini Lemon Poppy Seed Drizzle
        Cakes, 148
    Mini Red Velvet Cupcakes with
        Cream Cheese Frosting, 38
    Passion Fruit Cupcakes with
        Coconut Frosting, 44–46
    Piñata Cupcakes, 78
    Pumpkin Chocolate Chip
        Cupcakes, 111
    Strawberry Cheesecake
        Cupcakes, 39
Curd
    Lemon Curd, 177
    Lime Curd, 177
    Meyer Lemon Curd, 177
Currants
    Hot Cross Buns, 26
    Spiced Apple Strudel, 146
    Steamed Figgy Pudding, 152

d

Dates
    Sticky Toffee Pudding, 153
Devil's Food Chocolate
    Cupcakes, 112
Dulce de Leche Alfajores, 59

e

Espresso and coffee
   Chocolate Espresso Heart
      Cake, 150
   Mocha Bûche de Noël, 151
   Mocha Buttercream, 175

f

Figgy Pudding, Steamed, 152
Filo dough
   Honey Pistachio Baklava, 69
   Spiced Apple Strudel, 146
Flaky Pie Dough, Double Crust, 166
Flaky Pie Dough, Single Crust, 166
Flan, Caramel Orange, 63
Florentines, Chocolate, 155
Fluffy Vanilla Frosting, 171
Frosting
   Chocolate Frosting, 172
   Coconut Buttercream, 175
   Cream Cheese Frosting, 173
   Fluffy Vanilla Frosting, 171
   Fudge Frosting, 171
   Mocha Buttercream, 175
   Quick Vanilla Buttercream, 174
   Vanilla Meringue Buttercream, 174
   Whipped Honey Frosting, 173
   White Chocolate Frosting, 172
   White Chocolate–Peppermint
      Frosting, 172
Fruits. *See also* Berries; *specific*
   fruits
   dried, plumping, 13
   seasonal, 13

stone, types of, 13
   Summer Fruit Trifle, 85
Fudge, S'mores, 136
Fudge Frosting, 171

g

Ganache, Chocolate, 169
Ginger
   Apple-Ginger Tart with Cider-
      Bourbon Sauce, 104
   Caramelized Pear Ginger
      Cake, 94
   Gingerbread Cutout Cookies, 132
   Gingersnap Crust, 169
   Lemon Meringue Pie with
      Gingersnap Crust, 70
Gingerbread Cutout Cookies, 132
Gingersnap Crust, 169
Graham crackers
   Blueberry Cheesecake Squares
      with Hazelnut Crust, 64
   Honey-Nectarine Cheesecake, 74
   S'mores Fudge, 136
   Strawberry Cheesecake
      Cupcakes, 39
Grasshopper Pie, White
   Chocolate, 103

h

Hazelnuts
   Blueberry Cheesecake Squares
      with Hazelnut Crust, 64

   Chocolate, Cherry & Hazelnut
      Biscotti, 101
Honey
   Honey-Nectarine Cheesecake, 74
   Honey-Nut Pie, 106
   Honey Pistachio Baklava, 69
   Whipped Honey Frosting, 173
Hot Cocoa Cookies, 127
Hot Cross Buns, 26

i

Ice Cream, Chocolate Mint Chip,
   Cake, 79
Icing
   Royal Icing, 170
   Vanilla Icing, 170

k

King Cake, 53

l

Lavender Shortbread, 18
Lemon
   Hot Cross Buns, 26
   Lemon Crinkle Cookies, 58
   Lemon Curd, 177
   Lemon Meringue Pie with
      Gingersnap Crust, 70
   Meyer Lemon Curd, 177

Meyer Lemon Curd Pavlova with
    Blood Oranges & Cream, 125
Mini Lemon Poppy Seed Drizzle
    Cakes, 148
Panettone, 160–61
Lime
    Coconut Lime Curd Layer
        Cake, 42–43
    Lime Curd, 177
    Lime Curd Coconut Bars, 61
Linzer Heart Cookies, Raspberry, 138

m

Macarons, Peppermint Swirl, 130–31
Macaroons, Chocolate-Dipped
    Coconut-Almond, 20
Maple Pumpkin Pie, 98
Marshmallows
    Hot Cocoa Cookies, 127
    S'mores Fudge, 136
Mexican Wedding Cookies, 23
Meyer Lemon Curd, 177
Meyer Lemon Curd Pavlova with
    Blood Oranges & Cream, 125
Mini Cream Scones with Fresh
    Strawberry Jam, 25
Mini Lemon Poppy Seed Drizzle
    Cakes, 148
Mini Red Velvet Cupcakes with
    Cream Cheese Frosting, 38
Mint
    Chocolate Mint Chip Ice Cream
        Cake, 79
    Peppermint Bark Brownies, 128
    Peppermint Swirl
        Macarons, 130–31
    White Chocolate Grasshopper
        Pie, 103

White Chocolate–Peppermint
    Frosting, 172
Mocha Bûche de Noël, 151
Mocha Buttercream, 175
Muffins, Summer Peach-
    Raspberry, 80

n

Nectarine-Honey Cheesecake, 74
Nuts. *See also* Almonds; Pecans;
    Pistachios
    Blueberry Cheesecake Squares
        with Hazelnut Crust, 64
    Chestnut Torte with Mocha
        Buttercream, 140
    Chocolate, Cherry & Hazelnut
        Biscotti, 101
    Honey-Nut Pie, 106

o

Oatmeal Pear Crisp, 95
Oats
    Apricot-Almond Crisp, 66
    Oatmeal Pear Crisp, 95
    Plum Jam Oatmeal Streusel
        Bars, 62
Orange Marmalade, Bread &
    Butter Pudding with, 114
Oranges
    Blood Orange Tartlets, 147
    Caramel Orange Flan, 63
    Hot Cross Buns, 26
    Meyer Lemon Curd Pavlova with
        Blood Oranges & Cream, 125

Orange Vanilla Bean Sponge
    Cake with Sugared
    Strawberries, 47
Panettone, 160–61
Spring Strawberry Tart with
    Orange Cream, 34

p

Panettone, 160–61
Passion Fruit Cupcakes with
    Coconut Frosting, 44–46
Pastry Cream, Vanilla Bean, 176
Pastry dough
    Cocoa Tart Dough, 167
    Cream Cheese Tartlet Dough, 168
    Flaky Pie Dough, Double
        Crust, 166
    Flaky Pie Dough, Single Crust, 166
    Tart Dough, 167
Pastry Wreath, Chocolate-
    Hazelnut, 137
Pavlova, Meyer Lemon Curd, with
    Blood Oranges & Cream, 125
Peaches
    Peach Streusel Pie, 67
    Summer Peach-Raspberry
        Muffins, 80
Pears, 13
    Caramelized Pear Ginger
        Cake, 94
    Oatmeal Pear Crisp, 95
    Pear-Almond Custard
        Tart, 142–43
Pecans
    Classic Pecan Pie, 102
    Pumpkin Coffee Cake with Pecan
        Streusel, 118

Strawberry-Pecan
    Thumbprints, 19
Sweet Potato Pie with Pecan
    Streusel, 141
Peppermint
    Peppermint Bark Brownies, 128
    Peppermint Swirl
        Macarons, 130–31
    White Chocolate–Peppermint
        Frosting, 172
Pie dough
    Flaky Pie Dough, Double
        Crust, 166
    Flaky Pie Dough, Single Crust, 166
Pies
    Butterscotch-Bourbon Pie, 109
    Cherry Lattice Pie, 71
    Classic Pecan Pie, 102
    Honey-Nut Pie, 106
    Lemon Meringue Pie with
        Gingersnap Crust, 70
    Maple Pumpkin Pie, 98
    Peach Streusel Pie, 67
    Sour Cherry Pot Pies, 36
    Sweet Potato Pie with Pecan
        Streusel, 141
    White Chocolate Grasshopper
        Pie, 103
Piñata Cupcakes, 78
Pistachios
    Apricot-Pistachio Rugelach, 22
    Honey Pistachio Baklava, 69
    Pistachio Brittle, 96
    Plum Jam Oatmeal Streusel
        Bars, 62
Poppy Seed Lemon Drizzle Cakes,
    Mini, 148
Pot Pies, Sour Cherry, 36

Pudding
    Bread & Butter Pudding with
        Orange Marmalade, 114
    Steamed Figgy Pudding, 152
    Sticky Toffee Pudding, 153
Puff pastry
    Chocolate-Hazelnut Pastry
        Wreath, 137
    Rhubarb Turnovers, 28
    Sour Cherry Pot Pies, 36
Pumpkin
    Maple Pumpkin Pie, 98
    Pumpkin Chocolate Chip
        Cupcakes, 111
    Pumpkin Coffee Cake with Pecan
        Streusel, 118
    Pumpkin Whoopie Pies, 93

q

Quick Vanilla Buttercream, 174

r

Raisins
    Panettone, 160–61
Raspberries. *See also*
    Raspberry jam
    Chocolate, Raspberry & Toasted
        Almond Bark, 133
    Chocolate-Raspberry Mini
        Tarts, 135
    Summer Peach-Raspberry
        Muffins, 80
Raspberry jam
    Almond-Jam Cakes, 110

Chocolate-Raspberry Mini
    Tarts, 135
Raspberry Linzer Heart
    Cookies, 138
Triple-Decker Birthday Cake, 88
Red, White & Blue Bundt Cake, 87
Red Velvet Cupcakes, Mini, with
    Cream Cheese Frosting, 38
Rhubarb
    Angel Food Cake with
        Strawberry-Rhubarb
        Compote, 50–51
    Rhubarb Turnovers, 28
    Strawberry-Rhubarb Breakfast
        Cake, 35
Rolls, Cinnamon, 120
Rose & Vanilla Tea Cakes, 27
Royal Icing, 170
Rugelach, Apricot-Pistachio, 22

s

Scones, Mini Cream, with Fresh
    Strawberry Jam, 25
Shortbread, Lavender, 18
Shortcakes, Strawberry, 77
S'mores Fudge, 136
Sour Cherry Pot Pies, 36
Spiced Apple Honey Cake, 156
Spiced Apple Strudel, 146
Steamed Figgy Pudding, 152
Sticky Toffee Pudding, 153
Strawberries. *See also*
    Strawberry jam
    Angel Food Cake with
        Strawberry-Rhubarb
        Compote, 50–51

Orange Vanilla Bean Sponge
Cake with Sugared
Strawberries, 47
Spring Strawberry Tart with
Orange Cream, 34
Strawberry-Rhubarb Breakfast
Cake, 35
Strawberry Shortcakes, 77
Strawberry jam
Mini Cream Scones with Fresh
Strawberry Jam, 25
Strawberry Cheesecake
Cupcakes, 39
Strawberry-Pecan
Thumbprints, 19
Strudel, Spiced Apple, 146
Sugar Cookies, 164
Summer Fruit Trifle, 85
Summer Peach-Raspberry
Muffins, 80
Sweet Potato Corn Bread, 115
Sweet Potato Pie with Pecan
Streusel, 141

t

Tart Dough, 167
Cocoa Tart Dough, 167
Cream Cheese Tartlet Dough, 168
Tarts
Apple-Ginger Tart with Cider-
Bourbon Sauce, 104
Apricot Mascarpone Crostata, 33
Bittersweet Chocolate & Salted
Caramel Tart, 145
Blood Orange Tartlets, 147
Caramel Cranberry-Almond
Tart, 99

Chocolate-Raspberry Mini
Tarts, 135
Classic Tarte Tatin, 107
Crème Brûlée Tartlets, 41
Pear-Almond Custard Tart, 142–43
Spring Strawberry Tart with
Orange Cream, 34
Tea Cakes, Rose & Vanilla, 27
Tortes
Bittersweet Chocolate Almond
Torte, 49
Chestnut Torte with Mocha
Buttercream, 140
Tres Leches Cake, 86
Trifle, Summer Fruit, 85
Triple-Decker Birthday Cake, 88
Turnovers, Rhubarb, 28

V

Vanilla
Fluffy Vanilla Frosting, 171
Orange Vanilla Bean Sponge
Cake with Sugared
Strawberries, 47
Quick Vanilla Buttercream, 174
Rose & Vanilla Tea Cakes, 27
Vanilla Bean Pastry Cream, 176
Vanilla Icing, 170
Vanilla Meringue Buttercream, 174
Vanilla Ombré Layer Cake, 82–83

W

Wafer Cookie Crust, 168
Warm Molten Chocolate Cakes, 157
Whipped Cream, 176
Whipped Honey Frosting, 173
White chocolate
Peppermint Swirl
Macarons, 130–31
White Chocolate Frosting, 172
White Chocolate Grasshopper
Pie, 103
White Chocolate–Peppermint
Frosting, 172
Whoopie Pies, Pumpkin, 93

BAKING FOR EVERY SEASON

Conceived and produced by Weldon Owen International
in collaboration with Williams Sonoma, Inc.
3250 Van Ness Avenue, San Francisco, CA 94109

A WELDON OWEN PRODUCTION

PO Box 3088
San Rafael, CA 94912
www.weldonowen.com

WELDON OWEN INTERNATIONAL

CEO Raoul Goff
Publisher Roger Shaw

Associate Publisher Amy Marr
Editorial Assistant Jourdan Plautz
VP of Creative Chrissy Kwasnik
Design Support Megan Sinead Harris

Managing Editor Katie Killebrew
VP of Manufacturing Alix Nicholaeff
Production Manager Sam Taylor

Project Editor Kim Laidlaw
Art Director Marisa Kwek
Photographer Erin Scott
Photographer's Assistant Allison Fellion
Food Stylist Fanny Pan
Food Stylist Assistant Eliza Miller
Prop Stylist Emma Star Jensen

Printed in Italy

10 9 8 7 6 5 4 3 2 1

Library of Congress
Cataloging-in-Publication data is available.

ISBN: 978-1-68188-784-5

ACKNOWLEDGMENTS

Weldon Owen wishes to thank the following people
for their generous support in producing this book:
Lesley Bruynesteyn, Elizabeth Parson, and Rachel Markowitz.